Electrical & Electronic Projects

For Senior School Students

Nikhil Shukla

Published by:

F-2/16, Ansari road, Daryaganj, New Delhi-110002
☎ 23240026, 23240027 • *Fax:* 011-23240028
Email: info@vspublishers.com • *Website:* www.vspublishers.com

Regional Office : Hyderabad
5-1-707/1, Brij Bhawan (Beside Central Bank of India Lane)
Bank Street, Koti, Hyderabad - 500 095
☎ 040-24737290
E-mail: vspublishershyd@gmail.com

Branch Office : Mumbai
Jaywant Industrial Estate, 1st Floor–108, Tardeo Road
Opposite Sobo Central Mall, Mumbai – 400 034
☎ 022-23510736
E-mail: vspublishersmum@gmail.com

Follow us on:

© **Copyright:** V&S PUBLISHERS
Edition 2018

DISCLAIMER

While every attempt has been made to provide accurate and timely information in this book, neither the author nor the publisher assumes any responsibility for errors, unintended omissions or commissions detected therein. The author and publisher makes no representation or warranty with respect to the comprehensiveness or completeness of the contents provided.

All matters included have been simplified under professional guidance for general information only, without any warranty for applicability on an individual. Any mention of an organization or a website in the book, by way of citation or as a source of additional information, doesn't imply the endorsement of the content either by the author or the publisher. It is possible that websites cited may have changed or removed between the time of editing and publishing the book.

Results from using the expert opinion in this book will be totally dependent on individual circumstances and factors beyond the control of the author and the publisher.

It makes sense to elicit advice from well informed sources before implementing the ideas given in the book. The reader assumes full responsibility for the consequences arising out from reading this book.

For proper guidance, it is advisable to read the book under the watchful eyes of parents/guardian. The buyer of this book assumes all responsibility for the use of given materials and information.

The copyright of the entire content of this book rests with the author/publisher. Any infringement/transmission of the cover design, text or illustrations, in any form, by any means, by any entity will invite legal action and be responsible for consequences thereon.

Preface

V&S Publishers is pleased to bring out a new book – **Electrical & Electronics Projects**, that is designed for senior school students. The practical work helps the students in understanding the concepts in a systematic and scientific way.

The book consists of various projects that help students to learn advanced scientific principles and develop skills in science. Every project has been explained thoroughly describing all important aspects. The book includes projects that make use of electromagnetic forces, static electricity, current flow, motors and generators, resistance and capacitances, generating electricity, solid state electronics, and radio frequency energy. The materials required to do projects are commonly available at home or are easily available at minimal cost in the market.

The basic idea behind publishing this book is to provide students with the study material which is interesting, educative, and practical. With the help of this book the students can easily do the given projects and can think of doing other projects also. The contents are written in a simple and lucid language for better understanding of the concepts and explanations.

Thus, to gain inventive skills you need to go through the given projects, which will definitely prove to be a great learning experience for all of you!

Contents

100 W Inverter 9
Automatic Night Light 11
Automatic Water Pump Cut Off 13
Battery Charger 15
Battery Tester 17
Candles Go Electronic 19
Car Battery Charger 22
Continuity Tester with Melody 25
Electrical Machines 27
Electronic Door Bell 32
FM Bugger 37
Fully Automatic Emergency Light 39
Home Security alarm 42
Hot Water Geyser Controller 45
IC Timer Tester 47
LED Light Flasher 50
Multi Purpose Power Supply 52
OP-AMP Tester 55
Regulated Dual Power Supply 57
Single Pole, Double Throw Switch or 2-Way Switch 59
Staircase Light with Auto-Switch-OFF Feature 61
Temperature Switch 64
Touch Switch 66
Transistor Tester 68
USB Mobile Charger Circuit 70
Variable Power Supply and Charger 72
Water Sensor 74

Introduction

Welcome to the world of experimentation and practical science around us. In fact, science is the knowledge that is obtained through reading, experimentation, observation and realization in a systematic manner. Any performance done systematically is said to have been done scientifically. In short, science means a system which is enjoyable, interesting, and thought-provoking.

Electricity and Electronics

There is a very little difference between electricity and electronics. Generally, Electronics is considered to be a branch of Electricity. It deals with electricity since electrons move through electricity and are affected by certain devices like resistors, capacitors, coils, transistors, and integrated circuits. The human race has harnessed electronic power to perform various tasks such as to illuminate a light bulb, make a calculating machine called computer which can do mathematics operations at tremendous speed. Electronics is among the most rapidly changing sciences as various technological advancements are made every year.

In homes today you will find a wealth of electronic marvels such as computers, stereos, televisions, radios, telephones, laser music discs, copy machines. Electrical appliances such as washing machines, hair dryers, vacuum cleaners, toasters, microwave ovens, electric can openers, refrigerators, air conditioners etc. have enhanced our standard of living.

This book includes many topics and projects based on electromagnetic forces, static electricity, flow of current, motors and generators, resistance and capacitances, generating electricity, solid state electronics, and radio frequency energy. You have to only make your selection, and begin your project. Most of the materials needed to do projects are commonly found at home or are easily available at minimal cost in the market.

Aim of Experimental Study

An experiment is the base of the development and growth of science. In science the aim of experimentation is to verify a given law which has already been derived from a theory. New discoveries can be made while doing an experiment with open eyes and attentive mind.

Significance of Practical Work in Laboratory

Physics is an experimental science. From the past events, we find that most of the path-breaking discoveries have been made by scientists while experimenting on an already known fact. Though the theory is taught in the class, performing an experiment by oneself makes the taught principles quite clear. It is just like learning by doing. Practical works done in a laboratory provide young minds the systematic and scientific training. To avoid laboratory woks is just like to learn to swim without going to the swimming pool.

Features of the Book

This book deals with a wide variety of topics related to Electricity and Electronics. The scientific concepts and projects introduced in the book will help the students to understand advanced scientific principles and develop many skills in science, which are required to sort out everyday problems in our ever-increasing complex society. All the projects are classified into three grades (A, B, and C) for beginners, intermediates, and professionals respectively. In each project, complete theory has been described systematically covering all important aspects. We suggest making a 'schematic diagram' of each project, which shows a pictorial layout of an electrical circuit and the arrangement of components and their interconnection. This will enhance your display visually and comprehension as well. The book includes various activities which are useful for beginners and professionals i.e. it covers from the sixth standard to the graduate level.

Project-1

100 W Inverter

Can you design a 100 W inverter circuit ?

Introduction

Inverter is a small circuit that will convert the direct current (DC) to alternating current (AC). The power of battery is converted into main voltages or AC power. This power can be used for electronic appliances like television, mobile phones, computer etc.

The main fuction of the inverter is to convert DC to AC and the step-up transformer is used to create main voltage from resulting AC.

Materials Required

R_1	:	330 Ω, carbon film resistor
R_5	:	1 kΩ, carbon film resistor
R_{10}	:	250 Ω, carbon film resistor
R_8	:	1 kΩ, carbon film resistor
R_9	:	1 kΩ, carbon film resistor
BT-1	:	12V Battery
C_3	:	220 μF/25V
C_1	:	0.01 F
C_2	:	0.1 μF
D_5, D_6	:	Zener diode
D_2	:	LED
D_3	:	Diode (1 N4007)
SW-2	:	ON/OFF switch (SPST)
U_1	:	CD 4047 multivibrator
Q_1, Q_2	:	IRF 540 N-channel enhanced mode MOSFET
T_2	:	Step-up transformer

Assembly

As we see in fig 53.2, the battery supply is given the the MOSFET driver where it will convert DC to AC and the resulting AC is given to step-up transformer. From the step-up transformer we get the original voltage. As we see in fig. 53.1, IC CD4047 is a multivibrator with very low power consumption. It can operate in monostable multivibrator and also astable multivibrator. In fig 53.3, the given symbol is IC IRF 540 which is a N channel enhanced mode silicon gate MOSFET.

They are mainly used in switching regulators, switching convertors, relay drivers etc.

To Do and Notice

The main AC current is generated by the two MOSFETs which will act as two electronic switches. This AC is given to the step-up transformer of the secondary coil; from this coil only we get the increased AC voltage, this AC voltage is so high; from step-up transfArmer we get the maximum voltage. Zener diode help to avoid the reverse current. A heat sink must be added with MOSFET for better efficiency and good results.

What Happens?

12V battery is connected to the diode LED and also connected to the Pin 8 of the IC 4047 which is V_{CC} or power supply pin and also to pin-4 and pin-5 which are astbale and complement astable of the IC.

Diodes present in the circuit does not help to give any reverse current. LED works as an indicator to battery is working or not. Pin-2 is connected by the resistor and a variable resistor to charge the output frequency of the IC.

Remaining pins are grounded; Pin 10 and 11 are connected to the gate of the MOSFET IRF 540. The pin 10 and 11 are Q and ~ Q; from these pins the output frequencies is generated with 50% duty cycle. The output frequency is connected to the MOSFETS through resistor which will help to prevent the loading at the MOSFETS. The main AC generated by two MOSFETs is fed to the step-up transformer where we will get increased AC voltage.

Try It Yourself

Try to know how home inverter works.

Project-2

Automatic Night Light

Can you make simple circuit which make a light bulb automatically on when the day light fades into a dark night?

Introduction

This project needs an extremely simple circuit consisting of just four essential components to build a fully automatic self sensing night light. The light bulb used in the project could be the porch light that would go ON as the day light fades into a dark night. The same could also be used in the open terrace. There is a provision for disconnecting AC supply to the input of the circuit in case you deliberately want the lamp to remain extinguished during night due to some reasons or the other. One such instance could be when you are going out of the house during the daytime and you are not likely to return the same day.

Materials Required

R	:	10M Ω, 212W carbon film resistor
LDR	:	
SCR	:	Any 2A 600 V SCR such as OE 206, SN 206, 2N2601, TY6004
Triac	:	Any 2A, 600V Triac such as SPT 6M, 2N5757
Lamp	:	60W lamp
S-1	:	Mains ON/OFF switch
S-2	:	DPDT switch
Fuse	:	3A rating

Assembly

The circuit description is straight forward once operational principles of SCR and Triac are clearly understood. We know that an SCR is a three terminal device with anode, cathode and gate as its terminals. It behaves as an open switch as long as the anode – cathode voltage is less than the break over voltage of the device. An SCR remains in the open state when anode is negative with respect to cathode. Triac behaves like a combination of SCRs connected in inverse parallel with the result that for both positive as well as negative anode – cathode voltages, the triac can be made to switch to the ON state by applying an appropriate gate signal. Anode and cathode of an SCR are designated as MT – 1 (main terminal – 1) and MT – 2 (main terminal – 2) in case of Triac.

Automatic Night Light

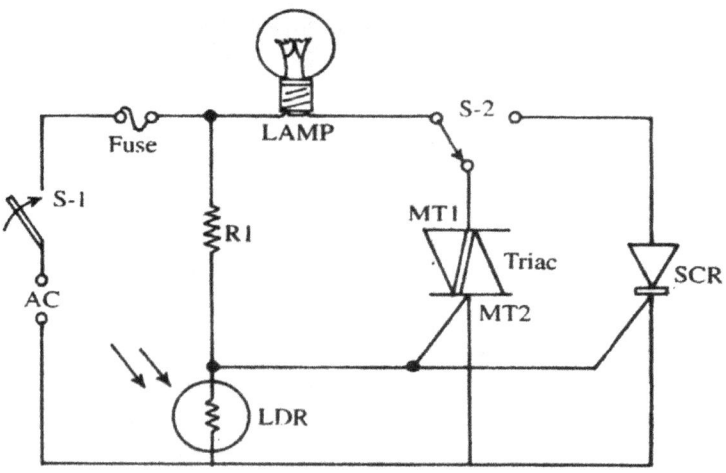

Fig. 2.1 : Circuit Diagram

To Do and Notice
1. Initially keep the S – 1 open and S – 2 in position – 1.
2. Place the circuit in a position so that light is falling on the LDR.
3. Connect the mains power cord and close S – 1.
4. The lamp should stay extinguished. It should not light up.
5. Now cover the top face at LDR by an opaque paper. The lamp should now light up.

What Happens?
Let us assume that DPDT switch S -2 is in position – 1 and it is day time. With sufficient light falling on the LDR, its resistance is very low, typically few tens of ohms. With switch S – 1 closed, AC voltage rises from zero to a peak value of about 330V during all positive half cycles across anode – cathode of the SCR. The same voltage after division by the potential divider formed by R_1 and the LDR appears at the gate. The SCR will remain in the open state as long as the gate voltage is inadequate to trigger it to the ON state. And this is what precisely happens during daytime when the LDR resistance is extremely low. As it becomes dark, the LDR resistance increases and at a certain point of time depending upon the darkness level, the SCR gets triggered and the AC input appears across the bulb and it lights up. Since in case of SCR, the SCR is active only during positive half cycles of AC, the bulb would give somewhat reduced light intensity. But then it gives you a longer lamp life and reduced drain on the AC power. There is no such limitation in case of triacs. You an notice a distinct increase in the brightness level of the lamp by switching S – 2 to position-2.

Try It Yourself
Make an SCR which behaves like closed switch, without increasing the anode – cathode voltage to the break over voltage.

Project-3

Automatic Water Pump Cut Off

Can you make an electronic device which controls the ON and OFF timings for a fixed duration?

Introduction

In multistoried complexes several flats are provided for residential and office purposes. In many cases, each individual house or flat has its own water tank on the top roof, sometimes several storeys high. Since water storage is a perennial problem, wasting any amount of water by overflowing storage tanks is unpardonable. The problem lies in accessibility of water tank for personal inspection and monitoring. An easy solution to the problem is to have an electronic device to operate the pump for a fixed duration and then cut it off.

Materials Required

- Transformer (T_1), bridge rectifier (B.)
- Filter capacitor (C_1), AC power supply switches (S_1, S_2)
- Relay switch
- LED
- Field-effect transistor
- Resistors (R_1, R_2, R_3)
- Diodes (1, 2)
- Capacitors (C_1, C_2, C_3) and connecting wires

Assembly

In the fig. 3.1 the circuit transformer T_1, bridge rectifier B and filter capacitor C_1 form the power supply for the electronic timer circuit. Switch S_1 controls power to the whole unit as well as the pump itself. Switch S_2 provides the option to operate the pump through the timer or bypass the time and run the pump directly through the AC mains.

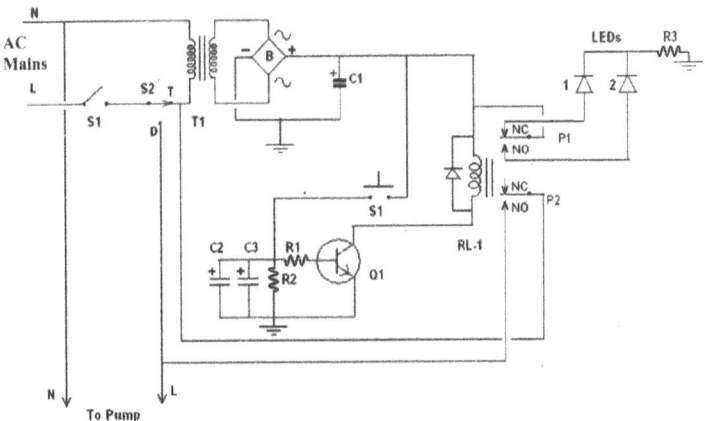

Fig. 3.1 : Circuit Diagram

To Do and Notice

Put the switch S_2 on the 'T' position, and S_1 close. In this condition the relay is not energized and the red LED is 'ON' through the NC contact of the relay.

When switch S_3 is operated momentarily, capacitors C_2 and C_3 are and charged up to the DC voltage from the power unit 6 volts in this case. The field effect transistor Q_1 conducts and the relay is switched-on.

This switches on the pump through the NO contact of the relay. This condition is indicated by the green LED switching ON, while the red LED switches OFF.

What happens?

The capacitors C_2, C_3 discharge slowly through R_2. When the voltage across the capacitors goes down below the required one to maintain the FET in the conducting mode, the transistor is cutt-off and the relay deeps back into its original position.

With the values of C_2, C_3 and R_2 given, the charge on the base of Q_1 is maintained for about thirty minutes. This can be increased by increasing the value of the C_2, and C_3 pair.

Similarly, the time period for operating the pump can be decreased by decreasing the total capacitance value. It should be noted that power to the pump is supplied through S_1, S_2 and the relay contacts, hence they should be rotated to carry the operating current for the pump.

Try It Yourself

Make an automatic water pump ON/OFF system for underground water tanks.

Project-4

Battery Charger

Can you make an Lead-Acid battery charger ?

Introduction

To charge a battery from AC, we need a step-down transformer, rectifier, filtering circuit, regulator to maintain the constant voltage that we can give to the battery to charge it. Suppose you have only DC voltage and want to charge the lead acid battery.

The main advantages of lead acid battery is its working efficiency and its durability. It can deliver high current at very low cost.

Materials Required

U_1	:	LM317/CYL voltage regulator
R_1	:	100 Ω
R_2	:	0.5 Ω
R_3	:	120 Ω
R_4	:	470 Ω
R_5	:	1 kΩ
D_1	:	LED
C_1	:	100 μF
C_2	:	0.22 μF
C_3	:	0.22 μF
D_2	:	Diode
Q_1	:	BC 547

Assembly

As seen in fig. 4.1, DC voltage is given to the DC voltage regulator LM317. The regulated DC output voltage is given to battery. There is also a trickle charge mode circuitry which will help to reduce the current when battery is fully charged.

Fig. 4.1 : Block Diagram of Charger for Lead Acid Battery

Battery Charger

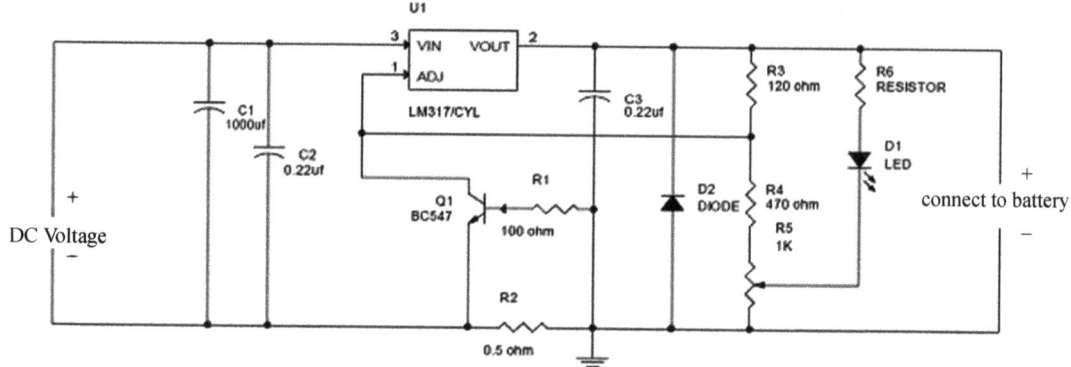

Fig. 4.2 : Circuit Diagram

As seen in fig 4.2 IC LM 317 is voltage regulator. The main function of this voltage regulator is to regulate the voltage and give the constant voltage without any noise disturbance. The maximum differential voltage for this IC is around 40V and also it gives exceeding output current of 1.5A for 12V to 37V. It has three pins input, output and adjustable pin.

Minimum voltage should be 18V which is given as input voltage to the regulator.

To Do and Notice

If the LED has glown, the battery is fully charged. When the battery is fully charged, the voltage regulator will reduce the charge current.

The battery should be charged with 1/10th its charging current. So, the voltage regulator must generate 1/10th of the charging current produced by the battery.

What Happens?

The DC voltage is connected to the Vin of the LM 317 and between these two we have connected the capacitor which removes the AC noise. The Vout of the LM 317 is given to the battery which is to be charged. Pin-1 is the adjustment pin of LM 317 and is connected to the transistor Q_1. Resistor R_1, R_2, R_5 will help to adjust the regulator. The output of regulated voltage and current is controlled by transistor Q_1 resistor R_1 and R_2 and potentiometer R_5.

Potentiometer is used to set the charging current. Resistor R_2 will have more current when the battery is getting charged. This will help to conduct the transistor Q_1.

Trickle charge mode : In this mode if the battery is charged the reverse current will flow. If the LED has glown, then we can say that battery is charged.

Try It Yourself

Design a charger circuit using SCR.

Project-5

Battery Tester

Can you design and build a battery tester to test dry cell and rechargeable battery with a voltage less than 2V?

Introduction
The objective of this project is to design a battery tester using LM 3914 IC that is able to test various types of dry cell and rechargeable battery with a voltage of less than 2V. The LM 3914 IC from national semiconductar senses the voltage levels of the battery under test and drives the 10 LEDs to ON or OFF based on the voltage that is detected. The current driving the LEDs is regulated by using the enternal resistor R_1 and hence limiting resistors are not required.

Materials Required

U_1	:	LM3914 IC
$L_1, L_2, L_3, L_4, L_5, L_6, L_7$	:	5 mm Red LED
L_8, L_9, L_{10}	:	5 mm Green LED
S_1	:	SPST toggle switch
R_1	:	1KΩ, 1/4W, 1% resistor
R_2	:	100Ω, 1/4W, 1% resistor
VR_1	:	1KΩ variable resistor
C_1	:	0.1 µF/25V ceramic capacitor
T_1, T_2	:	Probes

Assembly
The schematic shows the simple connections where the reference voltage at pin 8 of U_1 can be adjusted by adjusting the variable resistor VR_1. The voltage at pin 8 will set the maximum scale of the LED. In testing dry cell battery of 1.5V, set the voltage at pin 8 to 2.0V. Each of the LED will thus represent 200 mV when lighted up.

Test the circuit by using a breadboard before soldering the parts onto the PCB. This is to ensure that all the components that are used are in working condition.

To Do and Notice

Testing of reachargeable battery such as NiCd or NiMH is required, set the reference voltage to a lower value such as 1.5V as the typical voltage of a rechargeable battery is approximately 1.2V.

When testing the battery, take a note of the polarity of the probe to the terminals of the battery. T_1 is to be placed on the positive terminal and T_2 at the negative terminal of the battery.

What Happens?

A digital or analog multimeter that is set to measure the voltage of the battery is necessary. The voltage that is measured is used as a standard against the voltage that is displayed on the LEDs.

Try It Yourself

Know the applications of LM 3914 IC.

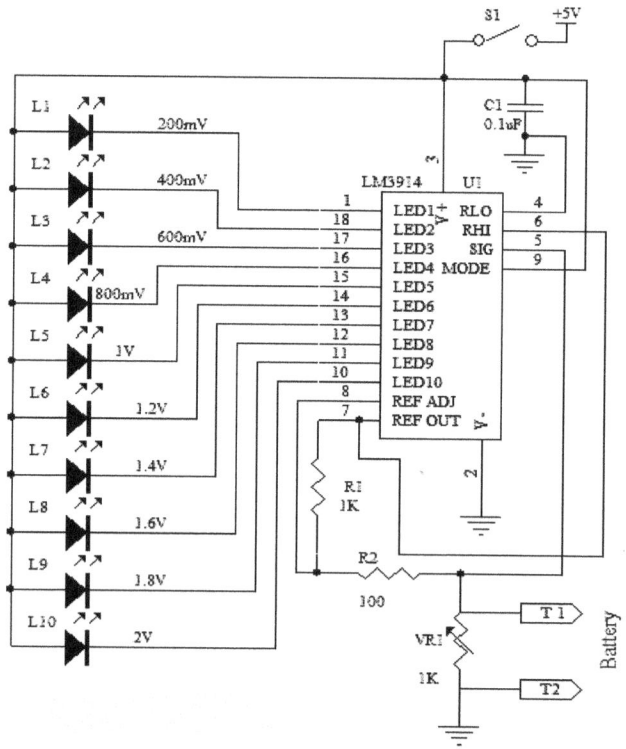

Fig 5.1 : Circuit Diagram

Project-6

Candles Go Electronic

Can you construct a simple project that can produce the effect of candle light (randomly flickering light) in a normal electric bulb ?

Introduction
This project is a simple circuit that can produce the effect of candle light in a normal electric bulb. A candle light as we all know resembles a randomly flickering light. We have to produce a randomly flickering light effect in an electric bulb.

Materials Required

R_1, R_2	:	10 KΩ, 1/4W carbon film resistor
R_3	:	180 Ω, 1/4W carbon film resistor
R_4	:	100 Ω, 1/4W carbon film resistor
P_1, P_2	:	100 KΩ, resets potentiometer
C_1	:	1 μF (tantalum) capacitor
C_2	:	0.01 μF (ceramic disc) capacitor
$C_3, C_4, C_5, C_6, C_7, C_8, C_{10}, C_{11}$	:	0.1 μF (ceramic disc) capacitor
C_9	:	1000 μF/25V DC electrolytic capacitors
D_1, D_2, D_3, D_4, D_5	:	1N4001 diodes
SCR-1	:	C106M or equivalent
VR-1	:	7805 voltage regulator
IC-1	:	555 timer
IC-2	:	76164
IC-3	:	7486
IC-4	:	7400
T-1	:	230V AC (primary) 7.5-0-7.5 V AC/250 mA secondary
L-1	:	Electric bulb, 40W to 100 W 230V AC
SW-1	:	ON/OFF switch

Assembly

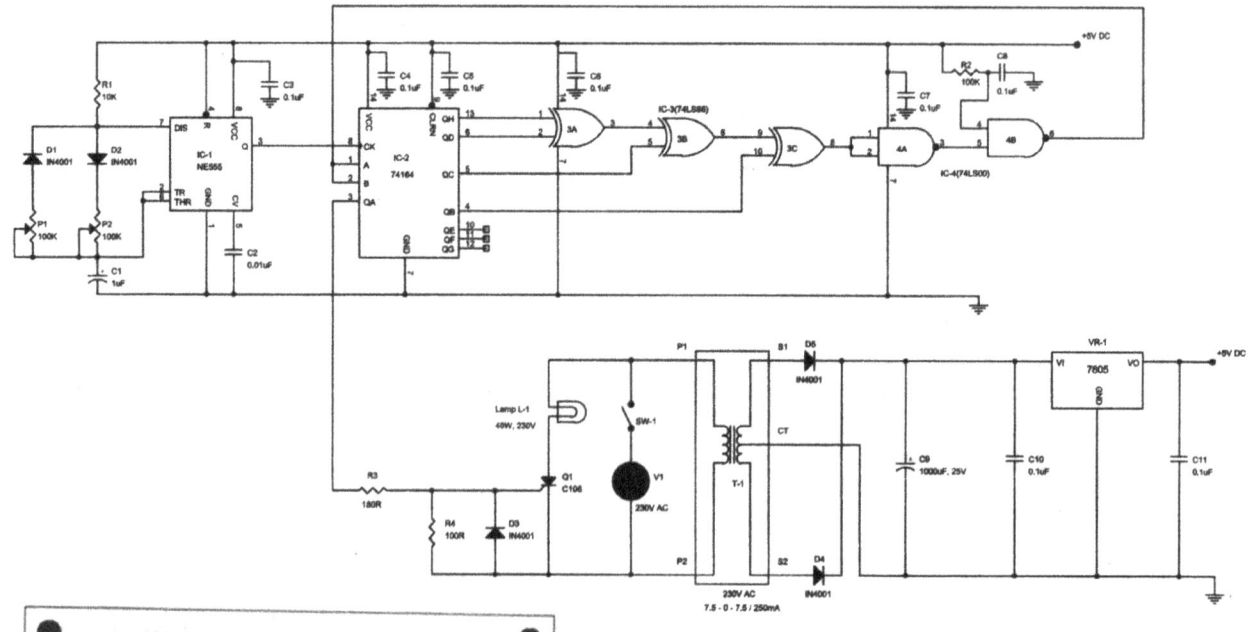

Fig. 6.1 : Circuit Diagram

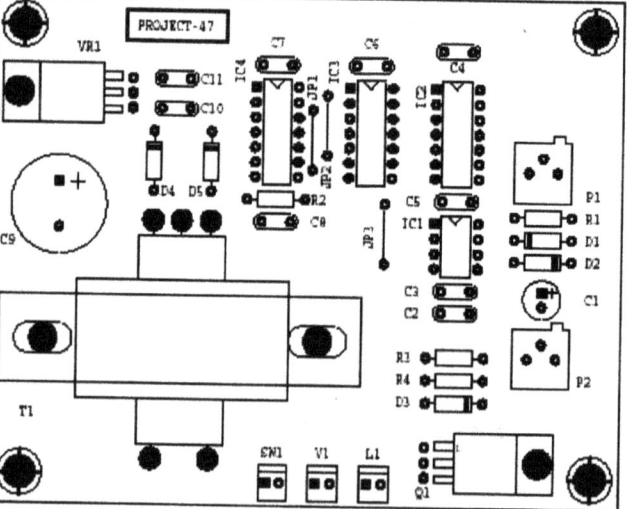

Fig. 6.2 : PCB Layout

Fig. 6.3 : Components Layout

Fig. 38.1 shows the circuit diagram and fig. 6.2 and 6.3 show the PCB layout and components layout respectively.

The circuit diagram is broadly divided into three parts. The first part comprises IC-1, IC-2, IC-3, IC-4 and the associated components generates a randomly changing train of pulses. The second part comprises an SCR, electric bulb in its anode circuit and gate trigger circuit components is basically a half wave AC power control circuit which controls the AC power being supplied to the electric bulb. The third part comprising diode D_3 (acting as half wave rectifier), the associated filter capacitors and voltage regulator VR-1 is the power supply circuit that generates +5V DC from 230V AC mains for operations of random signal generator.

To Do and Notice
When SCR is ON during positive half cycles of the AC input. In this duration SCR conducts would in turn depend upon the triggering instant of the SCR, which is random. Thus, we see a flickering effect in the light output.

What Happens?
Looking at the random signal generator, the heart of this part of circuit is the 8-bit shift register type 74164 (IC-2). Different outputs of the shift register pass through a set of logic gates (IC-3 and IC-4) and the final output appearing at pin-6 of IC-4 fed back to the input of the register. IC-2 is clocked by an astable multivibrator configured around 555 timer IC. The clock frequency is set at 100Hz. It can be varied a bit around 100 Hz. It can varieda bit around $100H_z$ to get the best flickering effect. The random signal triggers the gate of SCR. The electric bulb gets AC power only for the period for which SCR is ON. In the present arrangement, the SCR can be ON only during positive half cycles of the AC input. Hence, when SCR conducts we see a flickering effect in the light output.

Try It Yourself
Can you demonstrate the functioning of IC –7805 ?

Project-7

Car Battery Charger

How will you charge your car battery in the event of misbehaving or having become weak, what do you require in addition to 220V AC mains?

Introduction

A battery charger or recharger is a device used to put energy into a rechargeable battery by forcing an electric current through it. The charging protocol depends on the size and type of the battery being charged. Here is a simple battery charger circuit, the one that can be used to charge 12 V batteries of both the usual automobile type as well as the maintenance free sealed lead-acid type. The charger circuit described here is quite compact and can be placed right on the top of the battery required to be charged.

Material Required

- Resistors and capacitors
    R_1 : 2.2 K, 1/4W
    C_1 : 1000 µF, 25V (electrolytic)
    C_2, C_3 : 0.1 µF (ceramic disc)
- Semiconductor devices and ICs
    D_1, D_2, D_5 : BY 127
    D_3, D_4 : 1N4001 or equivalent
    IC-1 : 78T12 (it is 7812 in TO-3 package)
    LED-1 : LED (any colour)
- Miscellaneous
    Meter M-1 : Ammeter 0-3A (fig. 10.4)
    M-2 : DC Voltmeter 0-1V DC
    Transformer T-1 : 15-O-15, 2A
    Fuse F-1 : 1A tubular type with holder

Power supply terminals, solder metal, wires, main power ON/OFF switch.

Assembly

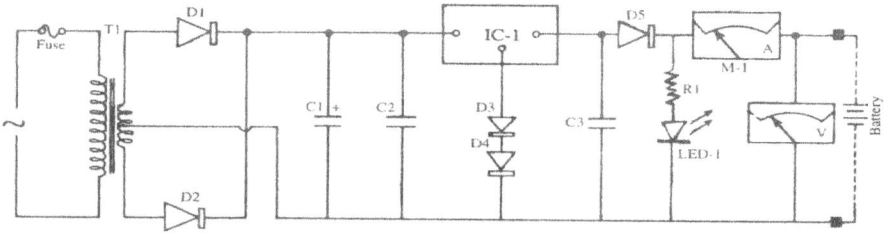

Fig. 7.1 : Circuit Diagram

Car Battery Charger

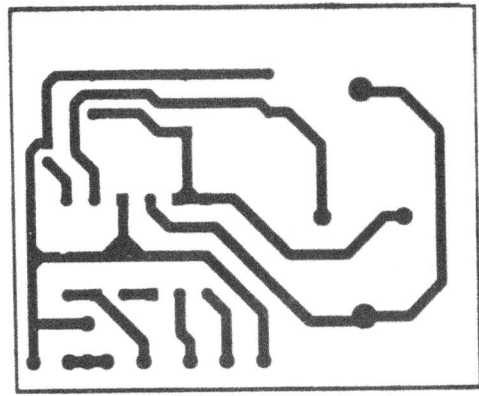

Fig. 7.2 : Components Layout

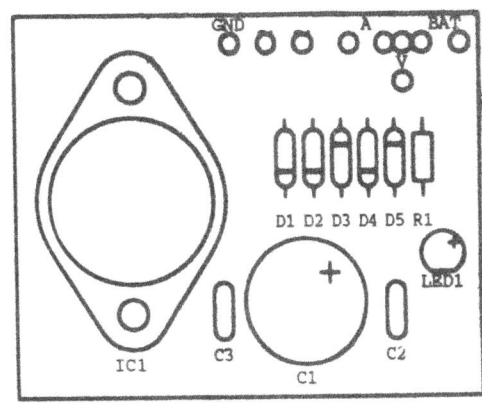

Fig. 7.3 : Lead Identification

Refer to fig 7.1 for PCB layout and Fig. 7.2 for components layout. Lead identification is given in fig 7.3, which shows the pin connection diagram of IC 78T12.

The circuit (see fig. 7.4.) is nothing but an AC/DC power supply that generates a regulated DC voltage of 13.2 volts from AC mains. Transformer T-1, diodes D_1 and D_2 and capacitor C_1, consititute the unregulated power supply portion with D_1 and D_2 alongwith transformer providing voltage transformation and rectification and C_1 providing the filtering action.

IC-1 is a three terminal regulator of the type 7812. The common terminal of this regulator has been lifted to a potential of about 1.2 volts by the forward baised diodes D_3 and D_4. So it gives a regulated output voltage of 13.2 volts instead of 12V which would be the case of the common terminal grounded. C_2, C_3 are decoupling capacitors. Diode D_5 provides the charging path for the battery. The charging current flows from the power supply to the battery. The doide D_5 also prevents the current to flow in the

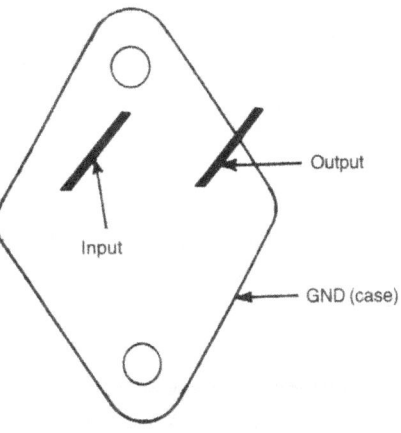

Fig. 7.4 : Circuit Diagram

To Do and Notice

Switch ON the AC power. Measure the regulated DC output voltage across C_3. 13.2 to 13.4 volts appearing across C_3 shows that the gadget is ready for use. Additionally the load delivering capability of the charger can be ascertained by temporarily connecting a 6 to 10 ohms (25 watt) resistance across the output in place of the battery.

Keep the gadget ON for a least ten minutes and see that there is no change in the regulated DC output voltage and also that there is no excessive heating of the transformer and regulator.

What happens?

When we connect 10 ohm resistance in place of battery, there is no change in output voltage of charger. It is the sign of good fitness of the charger.

Try It Yourself

What happens if the output of the charger is not regulated? What do you think if it is capable for charging the battery?

Project-8

Continuity Tester with Melody

How to design a circuit which can test broken wire i.e. continuity and undesired shorting of wires ?

Introduction

Many a times when we are connecting the components on the PCB or bread board, there is a possibility of compnents to get attached whether due to defects in the PCB or bread board or due to mistakes committed during assembling of the circuit. These defects are minor and superficial and are in the form of breaks in the wires. The small, inexpensive circuit of a continuity tester may be used to detect such defects.

Materials Required

R_1, R_2	:	1 kΩ carbon film resistor
U_1	:	IC 555
U_2	:	IC UM66 (music generating IC)
LS-1	:	Loud speaker 8Ω
Q_1	:	BC 107 transistor
C_1	:	0.01 8 µF capacitor
D_1	:	1N4728A capacitor
Battery	:	9V battery

Assembly

Here 555-IC works in astable mode of operation. 555-IC is designed to generate 2 KHZ output frequency. Output of 555-IC is connected to 8 ohms speaker. Reset pin is connected to V_{cc}. Here 4th pin is connected to ground through 1.0 KΩ resistor, so normally it is OFF. When probes connect to the testing point, 4th pin will get positive V_{cc} and speaker starts sound. Potentiometer helps to set the resistance to determine the point when the buzzer should turn ON.

To Do and Notice

If you want to check if the wire is connected from one end to another, then use the probes of continuity tester and put to the ends of the wires to be tested. If the wires are connected, then the circuit makes a sound indicating that the wire is continuous without any breakage in the middle.

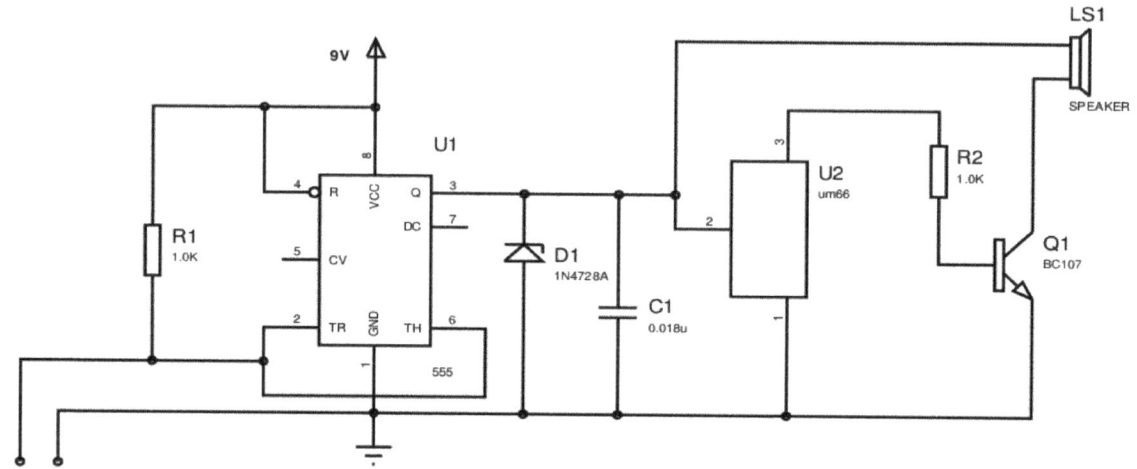

Fig. 8.1 : Circuit Diagram

What Happens?

The circuit uses 555 IC timer in buffer mode. The, output of the 555 IC is a DC voltage. When the circuit probes detects the shorted connection the output is given to a music generating IC which is UM 66.

The output is high only when the circuit detects that the probes are started. If not, the output is kept low. The music which is generated by IC circuit UM66 can be heard through the loud speaker.

The loud speaker is a mini 8 Ω loud speaker. A battery power supply must be used for powering this circuit.

Try It Yourself

Make a project which opens and closes curtain of your home and office by just pushing a switch.

Project-9

Electrical Machines

How do you bind a powerful DC Motor?

Introduction
In all rotating electrical machines an electromechanical energy conversion takes places. In all electrical machines, a charge in flux is closely associated with the mechanical motion to cause electromechanical energy conversion when electrical input energy is converted to a mechanical energy, the machine is called a motor. In simple words a device that converts direct current into mechanical energy is called DC motor. It is based on the principle that when a current-carrying conductor is placed in a magnetic field, it experiences a mechanical force whose direction is given by Fleming's left-hand rule and whose magnitude is given by gauge newton.

Materials Required
- Steel road 1/8" × 7" long
- 8 d common nails – 2½" long flat head type
- Nearly 20 ft., 22 gauge magnetic wire
- 35 mm film canister, rounded with cover
- Ply board 6" × 6" piece
- Two plywood boards 3" × 1" × (½)" pieces each
- Two fender washers, 1" diameter × 1/8" hole
- Steel pipe strap, 12(½)" long
- Two strong ceramic magnets
- Standard hook-up wire, 16 inch, 12 gauge
- Two alligator clip test leads
- 6 V lantern battery
- Duct tape, electrical tape, sandpaper
- Mini hot melt glue sticks
- Hand raw
- Drill
- Wire Stripper/Cutter with 14 gauge hole (to cut and strip wires)
- Aviation strips (to cut pipe strap)
- Bolt cutters (to cut steel rod)
- Pliers (to bend pipe strap)

- Hammer (to flatten pipe strap)
- Small flat head screw driver
- Mini hot melt glue gun
- Ruler
- Marker

Assembly

1. **Making the armature - An electromagnet on a stick**

    (i) Bind the 2 nails together head to tip using electrical tape, so that their opposite ends touch each other.

    (ii) Stick the steel rod between the nails sliding it exactly at the centre of the nails and glue in place with hot glue.

    Fig. 9.1 : Making Armature

    (iii) Fold the magnet wire in half and mark the centre with a piece of tape.

    (iv) Leave the first 12 of the wire free. Place the wire over the top of the nails just to the right of the steel rod, and wrap the wire away from you. Keep wrapping the wire back and forth staying on the right side of the nails until you get to the centre of the wire. Now, flip the nails around and continue wrapping of the wire. Be sure to leave the last 12 of wire free at the end of the coil.

    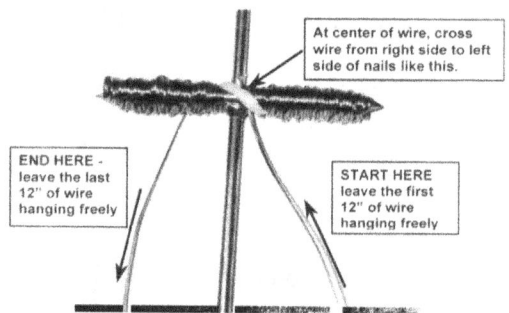

    Fig. 9.2 : Wrapping the Electromagnet

    The two ends of the wire coil that you left while wrapping are called electromagnet lead, because they lead electricity into and out of the coil.

    (v) Sand the insulated points of the magnet wire to make an electrical connection to the bare copper.

    (vi) Testing of electromagnet : Connect the sanded leads to the battery and hold each end of the electromagnet up to the same pole of a permanent magnet. If one end of the electromagnet feel attracting and other feel repelling. The repelling force is always weak; if it is not so, it means the turns of wire are not going in the same direction. Now carefully unwarp the wire of one side and rewarp it again with great care.

2. **Making the commutator :** The commutator is the part of the armature, it is just a switch for the electromagnet. It reverses the poles of the electromagnet from north to south and south to north in every half turn.

Electrical Machines

(i) The commutator in this motor is made is by folding the leads of electromagnet from 2 zig-zages. When commutator spins, the two zig-zags touch the brushes, which are connected to the battery, allowing the electricity to flow into the wire coil. When electricity flows into the wire coil, it becomes an electromagnet.

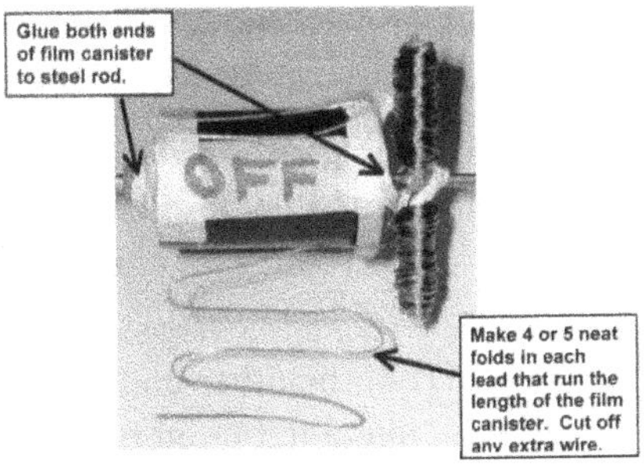

(ii) Using a nail, punch holes in the bottom of the film, canister, and in its lid, exactly at the centre.

(iii) Slide the canister onto the steel shaft until it is about to ½ inch away from the electromagnet, and hot glue it at both ends.

(iv) Hold the electromagnet straight up and down and place a piece of tape along the film canister on both the sides facing you and on the opposite side. These are the motors sides 'off spots'.

(v) Tape the folded electromagnet leads to the top and bottom of the film canister. The brushes rub against the leads to get electricity into the electromagnet, so be sure not to cover too much of the wire with tape.

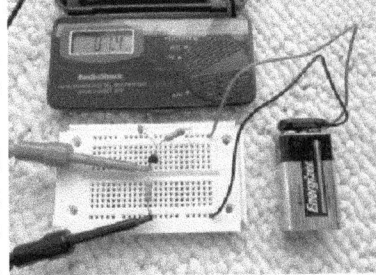

Fig. 9.3 : Making the commutator

Fig. 9.4 : A finished comutator

3. **Making the bearing blocks** : A motor must have bearings on both ends to hold the shaft in place and allow it to spin easily. For this motor, metal fender washers are used as bearings.

   (i) Cut 2 blocks of wood that are about 2"×3" × ½" thick

   (ii) Mark lines on the block 2" up from bottom to mark the height at which the holes will be drilled. On the front block, drill ¼" hole that is ½" in from the right side. On the back block, drill a (¼)" that is about in the middle of the block at a height 2".

   (iii) Now hot glue a 1" fender washer (with 1/8" hole) over the hole you drilled in each bearing block.

4. **Making the magnet frame**

   (i) Cut a piece of pipe strap that is 12½" long. Remove the corners.

   (ii) Make a mark 'A' that is ½" inch from the end of the pipe strap. Then make 3 more marks, B,C & D that are spaced at 3¾", 4" and 3¾" respectively.

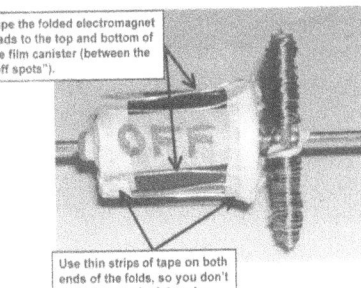

Fig. 9.5 : Making the Magnet Frame

5. **Making the Brushes** : The brushes in a motor are attached to battery and they are used to get electricity into the wire coil, turning it into an electromagnet. When the leads of electromagnet are touching the 2 brushes, the electricity flows into and out of the wire

coil, and whenever the brushes are touching the masking tape spaces (the off; spots) no electricity can flow into the coil, and the electromagnet will be off.

(i) Take two pieces of the standard wire, each 8 inches long

(ii) On one end of each wire, strip off 1 inch of insulation, and twist the strands so they are tight. These ends of the brushes will be connected to the battery using the alligator clip test leads.

(iii) On the other end of each wire, strip off 2 inches of insulation and spread them out so like a flat point brush.

6. Assembly of Motor Parts

(i) Slide the armature in place and also the back bearing block. Adjust the spacing of the brearing blocks so there is about 2-3" between the electromagnet and the front block. Make sure the armature spins freely and easily in the brearing blocks before gluing the other one down.

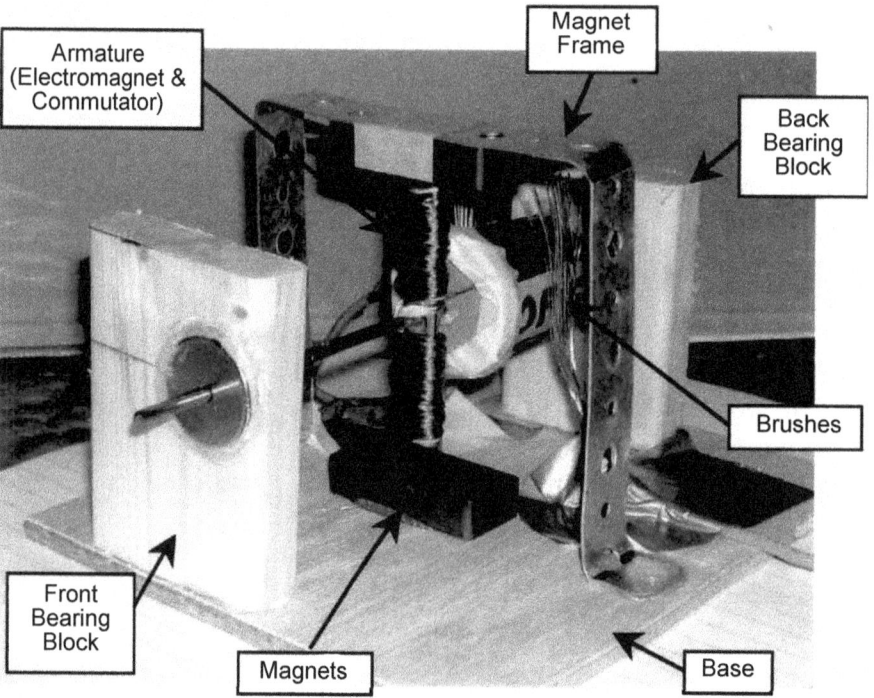

Fig. 9.6 : Circuit Diagram

(ii) Place the magnet frame directly over the electromagnet and hot glue it.

(iii) Place the 2 permanent magnets so that their opposite poles (N8S) are facing each other.

(iv) Place the brushes on the left and right sides of the commutator.

(v) Use the alligator clip test leads to connect the brushes to a 6 V lantern battery.

To Do and Notice
Give the electromagnet a little flick, and your motor will start up instantly.

What Happens?
When the terminals of the motor are connected to an external source of DC supply.

(i) The field magnets are excited developing alternate N and S poles.

(ii) The armature conductors carry currents. All conductors under N-pole carry currents in one direction while all the conductors under S-pole carry currents in the opposite direction.

Since each armature conductor is carrying current and is placed in magnetic field, the mechanical force acts on it. After applying Fleming's left hand rule, it is clear that force on each conductor tend to rotate the armature in anticlock-wise direction. All these forces add togegher to produce a driving torque which sets the armature rotating.

Try It Yourself

1. Take a ceiling fan's motor and understand its working.

    Hint : In ceiling fan's motor there are no permanent magnets. Then how it rotates.

2. Try of comprehend the commutator action in our experiment as well as in the motor of ceiling fan.

Project-10

Electronic Door Bell

How do we construct a 9-V Door Bell Chime using 555-timer?

Introduction

This door bell chime project is very low cost and affordable project that every beginners to electronic design can do. This is very simple wired door bell alarm that you can place on the door of your house. In most wired systems, a button on the outside next to the door, located around a height of the doorknob, activates a signaling device (usually a chime bell) inside the building. Pressing the door bell button, a single-pole single-throw (SPST) push button switch momentarily closes the door bell circuit and produces a signal from 555 timer at pin-3.

Materials Required

Label		Description
U_1	:	555-timer
R_1	:	15Ω ¼W, 5% resistor
R_2	:	15KΩ ¼W, 5% resistor
R_3	:	39KΩ, L4/4W resistor
R_4	:	68KΩ, L4/4W resistor
R_5	:	10KΩ, L4/4W resistor
R_6	:	10KΩ, L4/4W resistor
D_1, D_2, D_3	:	diode IN4148
E_1	:	47µF/25V electrolytic capacitor
E_2	:	470µF/25V electrolytic capacitor
E_3	:	22µF/25V electrolytic capacitor
C_1	:	15nF/25V ceramic capacitor
Q_1	:	NPN transistor 2SC945
Speaker	:	8µ speaker
S_1	:	Normally open-push button switch
BAT	:	9V batterry with battery holder

Assembly and Theory

This project is a wonderful application of 555-timer that is configured here in an astable mode. This project uses a 555-timer integrated ciruit. So, first of all understand the 555-timer.

The 555-timer circuit is a monolithic timer circuit capable to produce highly accurate and stable delays or oscillations. The 555-timer is used in many applications such as monostable and astable multivibrators, infrared transmitters, burglar alarms, etc. In addition to looking at its internal architecture, we will also consider two basic operational modes i.e. as monostable and astable multivibrator. But we discuss here only it's astable multivibrator mode only.

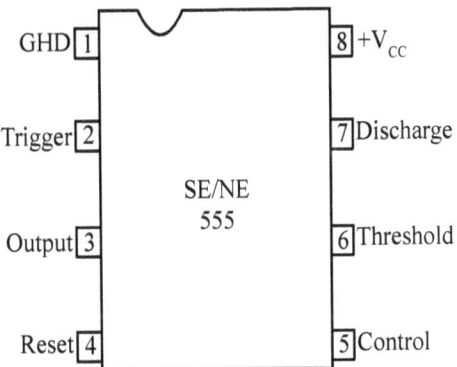

Fig. 10.1 : Pin diagram

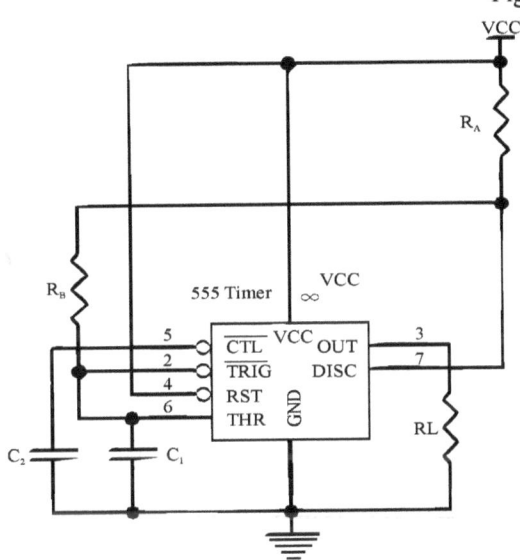

Fig. 10.2 : Circuit diagram of 555-timer

An astable multivibrator is a rectangular wave generating circuit unlike monostable multivibrator. This circuit does not require external triggering to change the state of the output. A 555 timer connected as an astable multivibrator is shown in the above fig. (10.2). The duration for which output voltage remains high or low is determined by externally connected resistor R_A and R_B and capacitors C_1 and C_2. Its output triggered continuously. The result of the output is a stream of clock pulses with a fixed pulse width and duty cycle determined by the resistors and capacitors connected to the I_C. When the output is high capacitor, C_1 charges towards V_{CC} through resistors $(R_A + R_B)$. When the voltage across capacitor equals $2V_{CC}/3$, the O/P switches across capacitor equals $V_{CC}/3$, which sets the internal flip-flop, with $\overline{Q} = 0$ discharge transistor is turned off and O/P goes high, the capacitor C_1 now charges through R_A and R_B. Then the cycle repeats. The related waveforms are shown in the figure below.

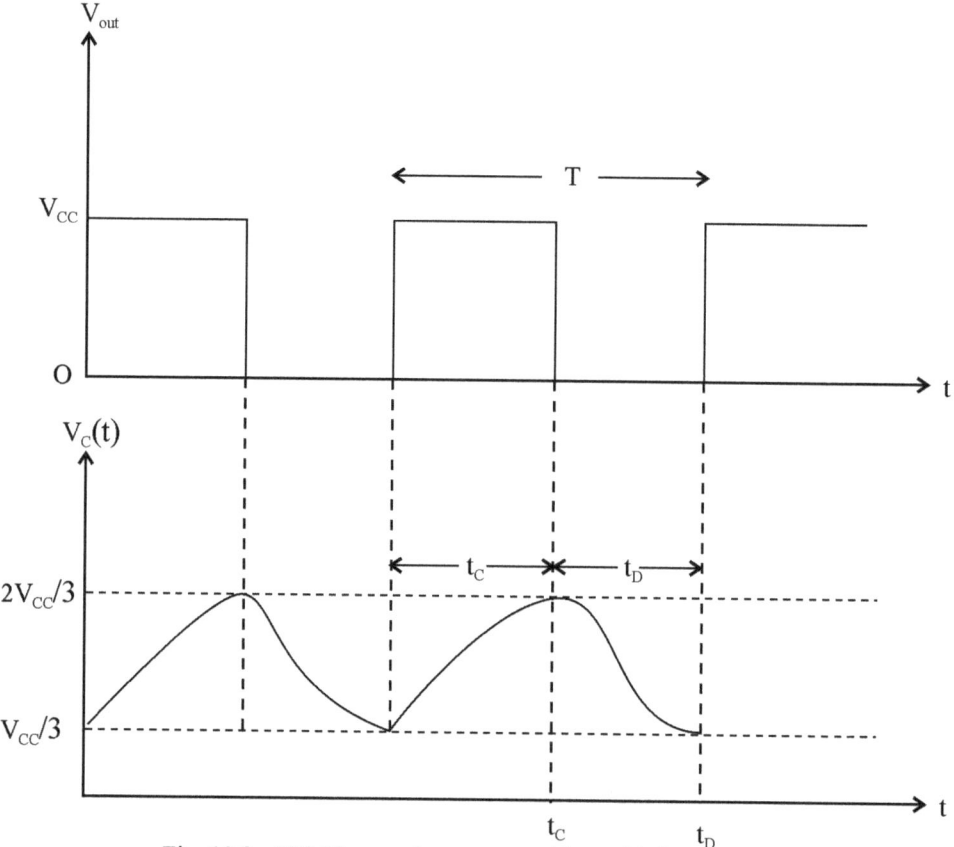
Fig. 10.3 : 555-Timer pulse as an astable multivibrator

A shown in fig. 14.3 during time t_c capacitor charges from $V_{cc}/3$ to $2V_{cc}/3$.
After calculations, we get

$$t_C = 0.69(R_A + R_B)C_1$$

and $$t_D = 0.69 R_B C_1$$

So, we can obtain the period of output wave from i.e.

$$T = t_C + t_D$$
$$T = 0.69(R_A + 2R_B)C_1$$

So, the frequency of the oscillations can be given by

$$f_0 = \frac{1}{T} = \frac{1}{0.69(R_A + 2R_B)C_1}$$

or $$f_0 = 1.45/(R_A + 2R_B)C$$

Here R_B = 68 KΩ
R_A = 68 KΩ + 39 KΩ = 107 KΩ
and C_1 = 15 nF
f_0 = $\dfrac{1.45}{(107+136)15\,nF}$
= $\dfrac{1.45}{243 \times 15\,nF}$

f_0 = 3.97 Hz

The duty cycle is given by

DHI = $\dfrac{R_A + R_B}{R_A + 2R_B} = \dfrac{175}{243} = 0.72$

DLO = $1 - 0.72 = 0.28$

The duration of the pulse is given by :

T_1 (High) = $0.693(R_A + R_B)C_1 = 1.82\,mS$
T_2 (Low) = $0.693(R_B + C_1) = 0.71\,mS$

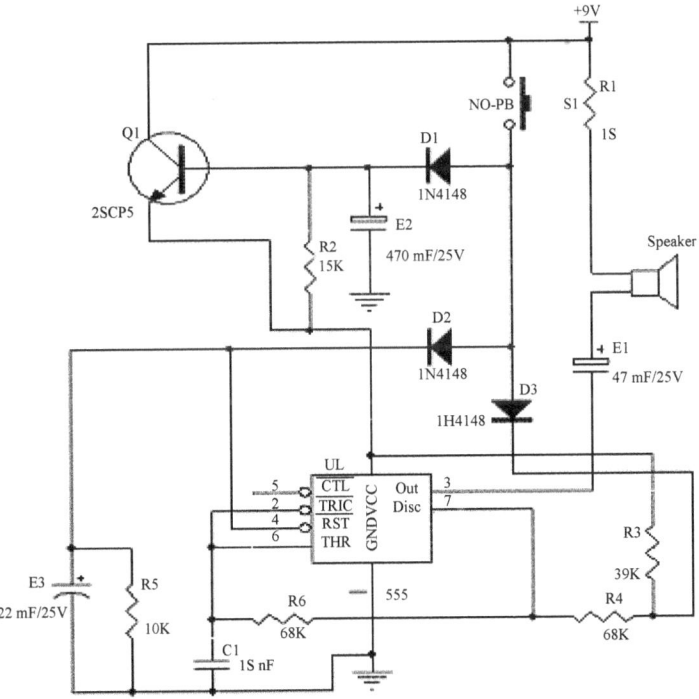

Fig. 10.3 : Door Bell Chime Circuit

To Do and Notice

When the switch S_1 is pressed, output pin 3 goes high for a time period already set by the values of elements. Now, this action gives a bell sound through the speaker.

What Happens?

When the output is high, capacitor C_1 charges towards V_{CC} through the resistors $(R_A + R_B)$. When the voltage across capacitor equals $2V_{CC}/3$, the output switches across capacitor equals $V_{CC}/3$, which sets the internal flip-flop with $\overline{Q} = 0$ and the discharge transistor is turned off. This cycle repeats.

Try It Yourself

Repeat the same experiment using the monostable operational mode of 555-timer.

Project-11

FM Bugger

Can you listen the conversation of another person from a long distance using the normal FM radio set ?

Introduction

Bugger is a device which gives information of one person to the other in remote location. Normally bugg is used to find out the status of a person i.e. where he is going, what he is talking etc. Here is a small circuit with which you can listen to another person's conversation from long distance using FM radio set. The FM bugger circuit is kept in room where you want to listen the conversation. The range of transmission area is around 100 meters.

Materials Required

R_1	:	22 kΩ, resistor (carbon film)
R_2	:	47 kΩ, resistor (carbon film)
R_3	:	330 Ω, resistor (carbon film)
L_1	:	Inductor coil
C_4, C_2, C_1	:	1 nF
C_3	:	4.7 pF
C_5	:	22 nF
SW-2	:	ON/OFF toggle switch
Battery	:	3V battery
C_6	:	50 pF variable capacitor
MIC	:	Microphone
Q_1	:	2N2222 transistor
Antenna	:	Dipole antenna

Assembly

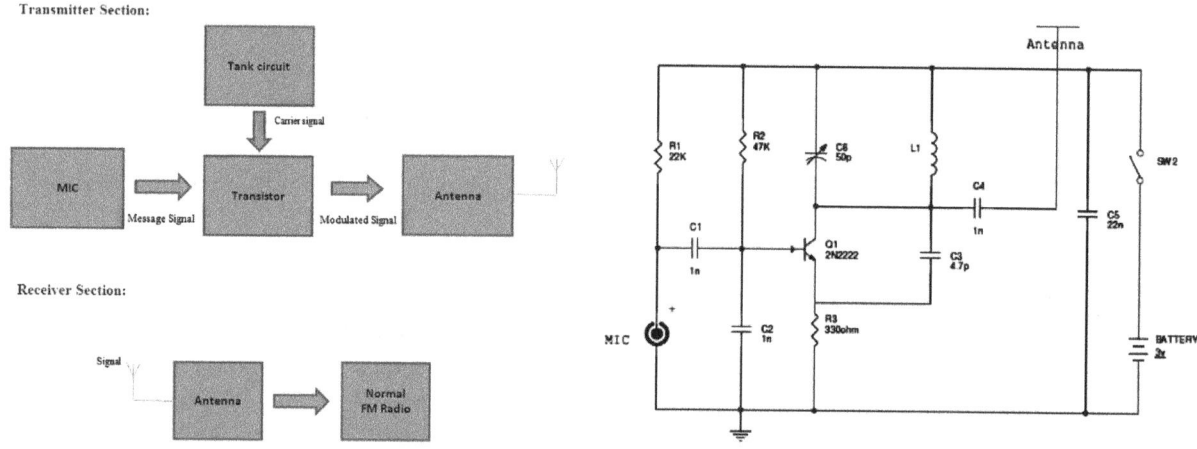

Fig. 11.1 : Circuit Diagram

You can make L_1 using about 25 cm length of 25 SWG wire wrap, the wire around a cylinderical object of 6 mm diamter and take it out after eight turns.

The circuit uses analog modulation in which the carrier signal is applied continuously to the message signal. Here, the conversation of people received by the microphone is given to the circuit and is modulated to the carrier signal and transmitted.

To Do and Notice

The FM radio receiver set is adjusted to your frequency for listening the conversion.

What Happens?

In this circuit FM modulation is used. In FM modulation, the frequency of carrier signal is varied in accordance to instantaneous amplitude of modulating signal.

Normal FM radio uses this type of modulation to transmit its signals. MIC will decode the conversation into signal which is given to capacitor C_1 where C_2 is used for removing noise and turning ON the transistor.

The tank circuit (C_6 and L_1) produces carrier signal for conversation or message signal. The transistor will amplify both signals and send it to air through the antenna. The capacitor C_4 removes the noise in the transmitted signal.

The capacitor C_6 is variable by which you can adjust the capacitor for producing your own carrier signal. The carrier signal should be in range of 89 to 105 MHz so that FM radio receiver set can receive your transmitted signal.

Try It Yourself

Make an automatic door bell with object detection.

Project-12

Fully Automatic Emergency Light

Can you build a fully automatic emergency light that remains OFF in the normal circumstances and switching ON automatically in the event of mains power failure?

Introduction

An emergency light is a battery-backed lighting device that comes on automatically when a building experiences a power outage. Such gadgets are very useful when used in places such as electricity meter box or the place where various cut-outs are located. The other useful places for these gadgets are dark corners where a little bit of light in case of power failure is of great utility.

Material Required

- **Resistors and capacitors**
  - R_1 : 27Ω, 1/2 W
  - R_2 : 470Ω, 1/4 W
  - C_1, C_3 : 0.1 µF, 25V (ceramic disc)
  - C_2 : 1000 µF, 16V (electrolytic)
- **Semiconductor devices and ICs**
  - D_1, D_2, D_3 : 1N4001 or equivalent
  - Q_1 : 2N2907
  - VR-1 : Three terminal regulator, type no. 7809
- **Other components**
  - S_1 : Main power ON/OFF switch
  - F_1 : Fuse (0.5 A rating) with holder
  - T_1 : Main transformer
    Primary : 230V AC
    Secondary : 12-0-12. 250 mA
  - Lamp : 6V DC lamp
  - Battery : 5 × 1.2 V, Ni-Cd cells

Assembly

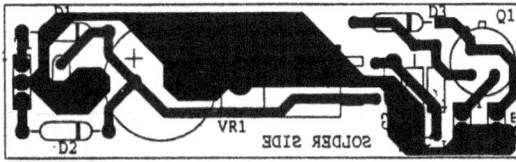

Fig. 12.1 : Circuit Diagram

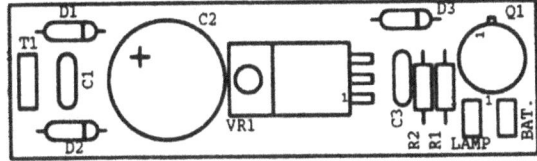

Fig. 12.2 : Circuit Diagram

Fully Automatic Emergency Light

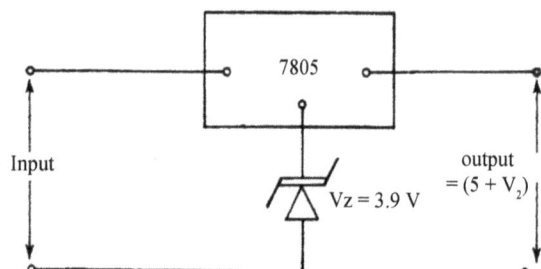

Fig. 12.3 : Circuit Diagram

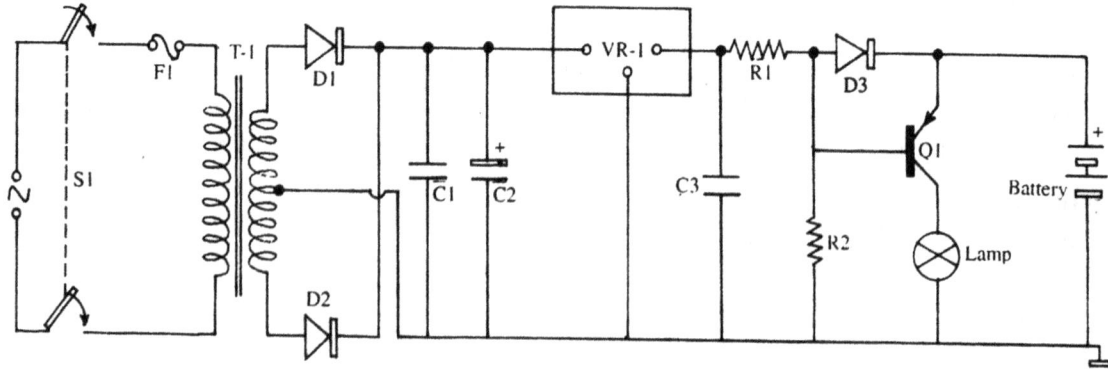

Fig. 124 : Circuit Diagram

Fig. 12.1 and Fig. 12.2 respectively shows the PCB layout and components layout. In case the three terminal regulator type 7809 is not available, as it is not a commonly used value, the same could be simulated from a 5V regulator (type 7805) as per the circuit configuration shown in fig. 12.3 What you have to do is to connect a 3.9V Zener doide from common terminal of the regulator to ground instead of grounding the common terminal.

In fig. 12.4 the circuit diagram of our gadget is shown. The circuit operates as follows : In case mains power is available, it is rectified, filtered and regulated to produce 9V DC. T_1 is the step down transformer, diodes D_1 and D_2 consititute the full wave rectifier alongwith the center tapped secondary winding, C_2 is the filter capacitor and VR_1 is a 9V three terminal regulator. C_1 and C_3 are decoupling capacitors. This 9V is used to provide constant current charging for the 6V battery (5 × 1.2V, Ni-Cd cells is series).

To Do and Notice

Diode D_3 is forward baised during charging. The forward baised diode D_3 ensures that the emitter potential of transistor is less than that of its base potential.

As a result, transistor (Q_1) remains in cut-off. R_1 is so chosen that the charging current for the Ni-Cd battery pack is about 100 mA. To sump up, in the presence of mains power, transistor (Q_1) is OFF and the battery is charged from the DC supply produced from mains.

In case of mains failure, the anode voltage of diode (D_3) falls below the cathode voltage of (D_3). D_3 becomes reverse biased, the base-emitter junction of (Q_3) is forward biased. The lamp is lighted.

What Happens?

When diode D_3 is in forward baised, the transistor Q_1 remains in cut-off and the battery is charged from DC supply produced from mains.

When diode D_3 is in reverse baised, the transistor Q_1 conducts. The lamp is lighted.

The lamp extinguishes automatically when the mains power is restored. The charge drained out of the battery during mains power OFF condition is now replenished again.

Try It Yourself

Make an emergency light that had similar application but has manual ON/OFF function.

Project-13

Home Security alarm

Can you build a security system for your home?

Introduction

A home alarm is a system designed to detect intrusion – unauthorized entry into a building. This simple stand alone home alarm project is a good project for those who are eager to know the concept of home security system. This circuit which consists of three 555 timers gets the input from a contact that could be connected to a motion detector or any momentary contact that monitors a certain process.

Materials Required

U_1, U_2, U_3	:	555 timer IC
R_1, R_2, R_4, R_6	:	10KΩ 1/4W, 5% carbon film resistors
R_3	:	82KΩ 1/4W, 5% carbon film resistor
R_5	:	200Ω 1/4W, 5% carbon film resistor
VR_1	:	1MΩ potentiometer
VR_2	:	200KΩ potentiometer
C_1, C_2, C_3	:	0.01 µF/25V ceramic capacitor
E_3	:	10 µF/25V electrolytic capacitor
E_1, E_2	:	220 µF/25V electrolytic capacitor
D_1, D_2	:	Diode 1N4003
SPKR (Speaker)	:	8Ω speaker
Q_1	:	Transistor TIP41A
S_1	:	SPST switch
CT	:	Dry contact to trigger the alarm.

Assembly

The circuit diagram of the project is shown in fig 13.2.

The first timer U_1 is configured as a monostable timer with a variable timing up to a maximum of 220 seconds. The timing can be changed by ajdusting the VR_1 1MΩ potentiometer. If you need to further increase the timing, the electrolytic capacitor E_1 can be changed to a larger value.

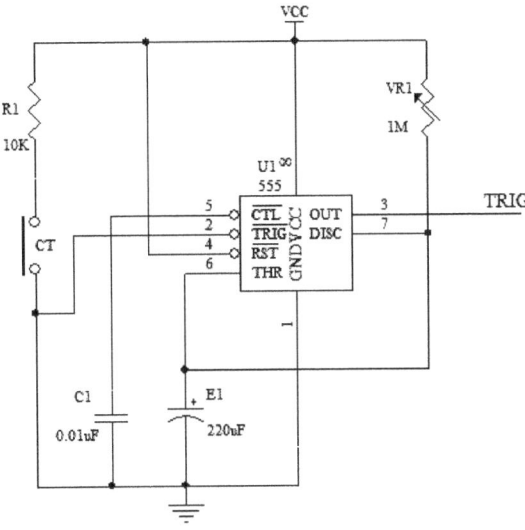

Fig 13.1 : Monostable 555 Timer

Once the contact CT is momentarily closed and a pulse will be generated at the output pin 3 of U_1. U_1 is then feed into pin 4 Reset of both U_2 and U_3 timers causing both timers to start their astable mode operations. U_2 is configured as a square wave close to 1 H_z astable oscillator by fining the values of E_3, R_2 and R_3.

$$f = 1.44/[R_2 + 2R_3)(E_3)]$$
$$= 1.44/[10 + 2*82(10)]$$
$$= 0.8\ H_z.$$

The output of U_2 timers is used to feed control voltage of the U_3 timer through register R_6 where it is subjected to frequency modulation. This frequency modulation will generate a tone similar to the police siren.

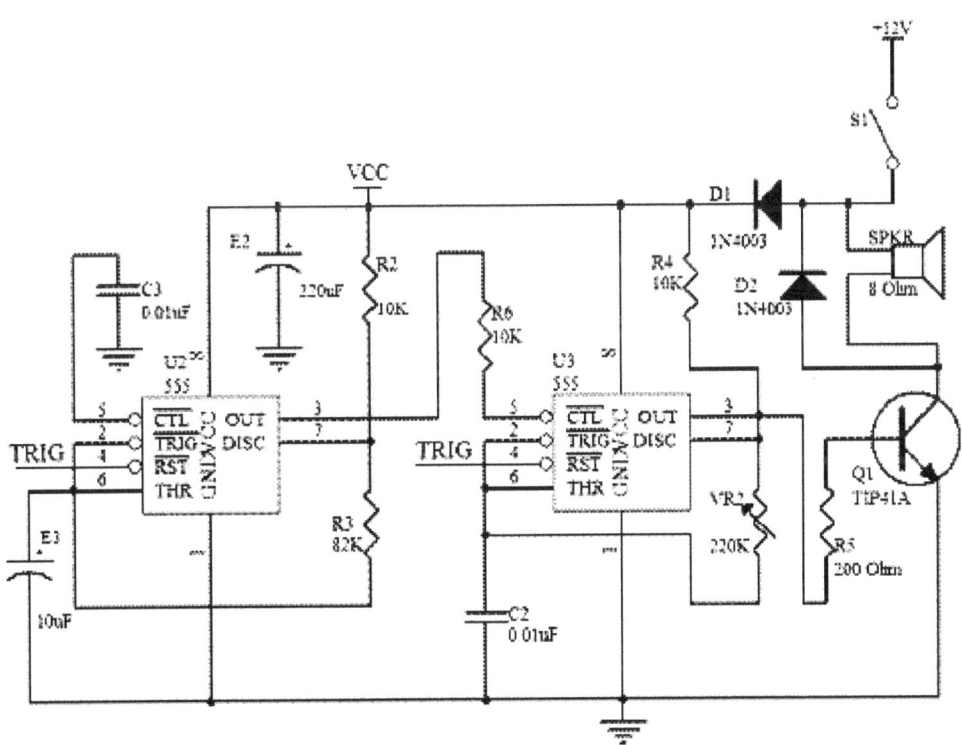

Fig 13.2 : Circuit Diagram

To Do and Notice

The output of U_2 is used to drive a power transistor which in turn drives 8Ω speaker. Diode D_2 is used to prevent the damage of transistor Q_1 due to the back emf generated by the speaker during ON/OFF driving of the speaker.

The frequency of generated tone can be varied by changing the value of potentiometer VR_2.

When set to its maximum value of 220KΩ, it will have a tone frequency of approximately 320 H_z.

What Happens?

Once the contact is momentarily closed, the first timer which is configured as a monostable output will output a high pulse with a duration upto a maximum 220 seconds. This output is fed into the second timer which is configured as an astable 1Hz square wave generator. The output of this second timer is then fed into the third timer to control its frequency modulation. This frequency modulation will then power a speaker and generate a siren tone similar to the police siren.

Try It Yourself

Make a simple laser based intruder alarm.

Project-14

Hot Water Geyser Controller

Can you make a circuit which turns a geyser OFF/ON when water gets hot and ready for bathing?

Introduction
This circuit is made to turn ON/OFF the geysers when the temperature of water reaches at desired value. This circuit has an inherent ability to detect the temperature and turn ON or OFF automatically.

This circuit has thermistor which is a temperature sensing element and helps the circuit to determine the temperature of the water.

Materials Required

R_1	:	120 Ω
RV-2	:	Variable resistor 100 kW
R_2	:	4.7 kΩ
R_4, R_2	:	4.7 kΩ
R_5	:	1.0 kΩ
R_6	:	56 kΩ
R_7	:	470 kΩ
R_8	:	100 kΩ
R_{12}	:	470 kΩ
Q_1, Q_2	:	BC 547 NPN transistor
Q_3	:	BC 107
RL-1	:	Relay switch
Battery	:	9V battery
TH-1	:	Thermistor

Assembly
The thermistor is kept in contact with water while assembling the circuit on field. Transistor BC 547 is a general purpose NPN transistor. Here, transistors are used as a switch. It drives the relay switch.

Hot Water Geyser Controller

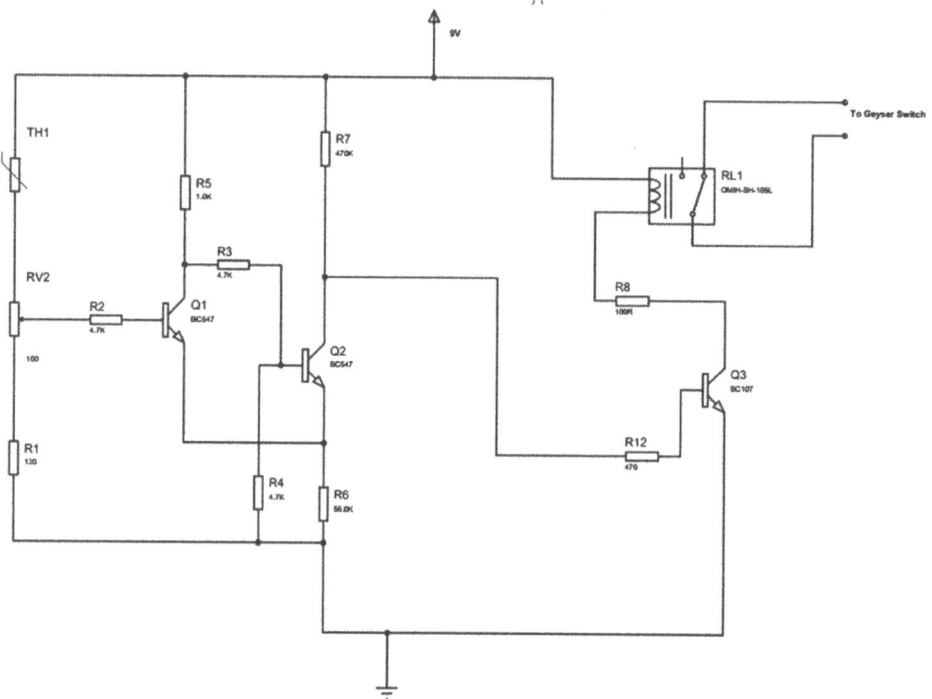

Fig. 14.1 : Circuit Diagram

To Do and Notice

When the driving transistor of relay is turned ON, the DC current gets passed through the relay which turns the relay ON. The relay is connected in normally closed mode in which it is normally closed and the circuit is opened when the relay is turned ON. When circuit is closed, the geyser in turned-ON and when the circuit is open, the relay is turned-OFF.

What Happens?

When the temperature is below the threshold value, the relay is OFF and the geyser will remain ON. When the temperature reaches the value equal to or exceeding the threshold value, then the relay turns ON which further breaks the connection and so the geyser turns OFF.

When the thermistor senses a low temperature, the voltage divider arrangement provides a low voltage to the switching transistor. Due to this, the transistor is in the OFF mode. If the temperatue reaches a value greater than a specific threshold, the transistor gets turned ON. As we have discussed earlier, the transistor acts as a switch and turns ON another transistor which drives the relay. When the driving transistor turns ON, the DC current gets passed through the relay which turns the relay ON.

Try It Yourself

Try to make an auto turn-OFF soldering iron circuit.

Project-15

IC Timer Tester

How can you differentiate between good and bad ICs for a particular gadget ?

Introduction
The objective of this project is to build simple and easy to use test gadget that can be used to identify good and bad IC timers from a given lot. This project not only enables you to test the IC timer 555, it will also give you an opportunity to appreciate the tremendous function potential of various terminals of the truly versatile IC. It practically tests the functionality of each and every terminal of the timer with the result that a timer declared fit by this gadget is good in the true sense.

Materials Required

R_1, R_2	:	22 KΩ, 1/4W resistor (carbon film)
R_4, R_5, R_{11}	:	3.3 KΩ, 1/4W resistor (carbon film)
R_6	:	4.7 KΩ, 1/4W resistor (carbon film)
R_7	:	47 Ω, 1/4W resistor (carbon film)
R_8	:	150 KΩ, 1/4W resistor (carbon film)
R_9	:	47 KΩ, 1/4W resistor (carbon film)
R_{10}	:	1 KΩ, 1/4W resistor (carbon film)
R_3	:	10 KΩ, 1/4W resistor (carbon film)
P_1	:	1 KΩ, (preset) potentiometers
P_2, P_3	:	100 KΩ, (preset) potentiometers
C_1, C_3	:	0.01 µF (ceramic disc)
C_2, C_6, C_7	:	0.1 µF (ceramic disc)
C_4	:	10 µF, 25V (electrolytic)
C_5	:	100 µF, 25V (electrolytic)
D_1, D_2, D_3, D_4	:	1N4001 or equivalent diodes
LED-3, LED-1, LED-2	:	Preferably of different colours
IC-1	:	CD4011B
SW-1	:	Microswitch
SW-2, SW-3	:	DPDT switch

IC Timer Tester

Transformer   :   14-0-14, 500 mA mains transformer
Fuse   :   1 Ampere
IC socket   :   8-pin dual in line

Assembly

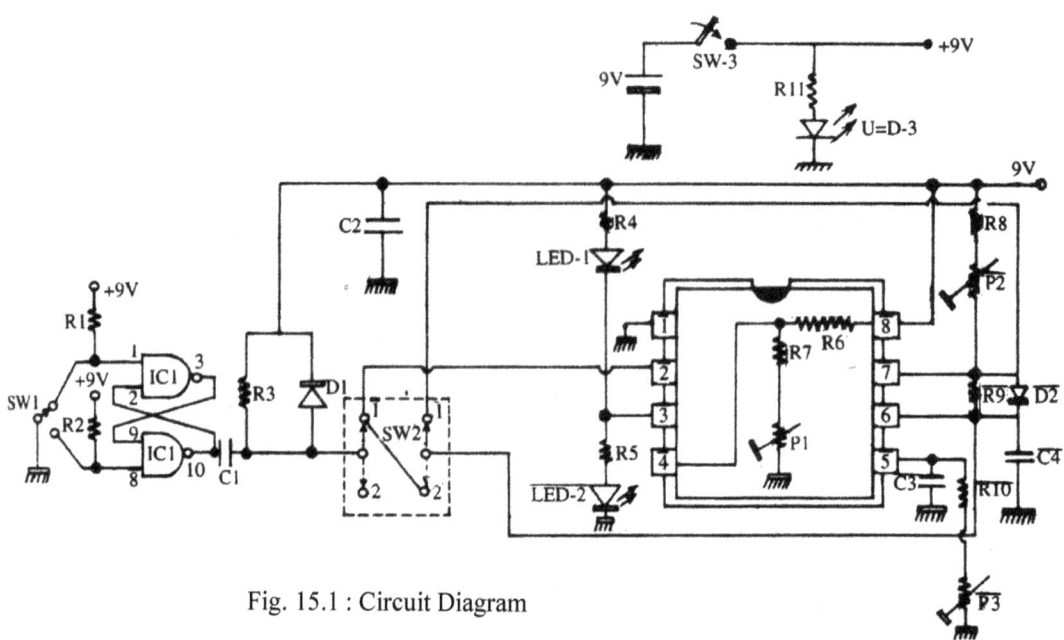

Fig. 15.1 : Circuit Diagram

The two basic configuration in which the IC timer 555 can be used are: (i) Astable mode of operation and (ii) Monostable mode of operation. When the DPDT switch (SW-2) is in position 1-1, the timer under test automatically gets wired as monostable multivibrator. In this case, the monoshot can be triggered by the micro-switch (SW-1). The debouncing circuit consituted by the two NAND gates of IC-1 produces a clean rectangular pulse from the pulse produced by pressing the microswitch. Resistor R_3, capacitor C_1 and the diode D_1 ensure that the tigger terminal of IC-555 (pin-2 is the trigger terminal) gets the desired V_{cc} to ground trigger pulse. This differentiator circuit pulse is less than the expected monoshot output pulse. Remember the trigger pulse width which is less than the expected monoshot output pulse which is an essential requirement of this mode of operaton.

When the DPDT switch is in position 2-2, the timer gets connected in the astable mode of operation. The output is a pulse train with the high time determined by the total resistance offered by the series combination of R_8, R_9, P_2 and capacitor C_4 whereas the low time is determined by resistor R_9 and capacitor C_4.

The RESET terminal of IC timer (Pin-4) should be tied to V_{cc} in the normal circumstances. More precisely, voltage at Pin-4 should be greater than 0.8V. A voltage of less than that resets the output.

Whether you have connected the timer in the monoshot or astable mode of operation, the output goes low the moment you bring the reset terminal below 0.8V.

The control terminal (Pin-5) can be used to change the high time or the ON-time of the output pulse train in the astable mode and the pulse width at the output in monoshot mode by applying on external voltage.

To Do and Notice

This project can thus be used to carry out the following tests which give timer-555

1. The timer IC can be checked in the astable configuration
2. The timer IC can be checked in monostable configuration
3. The capability of the reset terminal to override all functions and rest the output to low can be checked.
4. The function of the control terminal to change the ON-time or the High-time of the output waveform in case of astable mode of operation and the output pulse width in case of monostable mode of operation can be verified.

What Happens?

When the DPDT switch (SW-2) is in position 1-1, the timer under test is a monostable multivibrator.

When DPDT switch is in position 2-2, the timer gets connected in the astable mode of operation.

The control terminal (Pin-5) can be used to change high time or the ON-time of the ouput pulse train in astable mode and the pulse width at output in monoshot mode.

The pulse width in the monoshot mode is given by :

1.1 × (total charging resistance) × (charging capacitance)

This expression is valid when there is no external resistance connected from Pin-5.

Try It Yourself

Can you determine the high-time and low-time in astable mode ?

Project-16

LED Light Flasher

Can you build LED Light Flasher with two LEDs connected in parallel?

Introduction

This is a simple LED light flasher project that uses a CMOS 74CO4 IC to alternately ON and OFF two LEDs that are connected in parallel. The hex inverter MM 74CO4 from Fairchild Semiconductor has a wide operating power supply voltage range from 3V to 15V DC. It has a typical low power consumption of 10µW/package and has high noise immunity. It is back to back compatible with the standard 74 logic family which is freely available in the market. All its inputs have diode clamps to V_{cc} and GND which protect them from damage due to electrostatic discharge.

Materials Required

R_1, R_2, R_3	:	10MΩ resistor 1/4W 5%
R_4	:	510Ω resistor 1/4W 5%
C_1	:	0.1 µF/25V ceramic capacitor
S_1	:	SPDT switch
IC_1	:	MM 74CO4 Hex inverter
LED_1, LED_2	:	3 mm or 5 mm LEDs
9V	:	9V battery and battery clip

Assembly

The schematic above shows the simple configuration of the project. It uses two inverters U1A and U1B form an oscillator configuration where the frequency of the oscillation is given by

$$f = 1/[1.4\ RC]$$
$$= 1/[1.4\ (10MΩ)\ (0.1µf)]$$
$$= 0.7\ H_z.$$

The square wave frequency of $0.7\ H_z$ is used to feed the input of U1D which is used as a buffer circuit. At the same time, the other inverter U1C gets its input from Pin 2 and Pin 3 of V1. With this configuration, when U1D output is high, U1C output will be low and vice-versa. In this way when LED_1 is ON, LED_2 will be off and this will alternate at a frequency of $0.7\ H_z$. The current that goes through LED is given by

$$I = (9V - 7V/510\ Ω)$$
$$= 14\ µA$$

LED Light Flasher

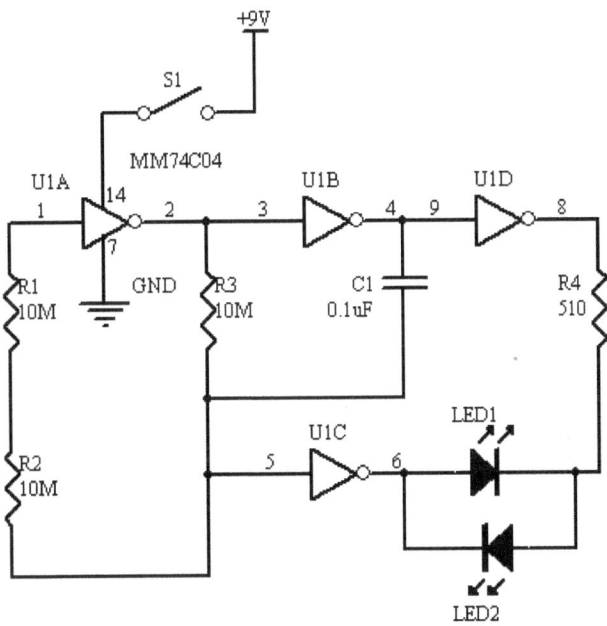

Fig. 16.1 : Circuit Diagram

To Do and Notice
We notice that when LED_1 is ON the another LED_2 is OFF and this will alternately occur.

What Happens?
It is assumed that the voltage drop across each diode is 2V when it turns ON. One can experiment with the oscillation frequency by changing the values of R_1, R_2, R_3 and C_1. The brightness of the LEDs can also be charged by changing the values of the resistor R_4. However, always ensure that the current through the LEDs is not exceeded or else the LEDs will be damaged.

Try It Yourself
Make 4 LEDs flashing alternately which is in series.

Project-17

Multi Purpose Power Supply

Can you make regulated and put DC voltages of 3V, 6V, 9V and 12V that are seleted one at time with the help of a rotary switch, from a single AC (220-230) source?

Introduction

A regulated power supply is one that controls the output voltage or current to a specific value despite variations in either load current or voltage supplied by the power supply's energy source. To produce DC from an AC powered supply, a rectifier is used to convert AC voltage to a DC voltage. Here we intend to build a multi-purpose regulated power supply that will serve as a very useful alternative to our multiple needs of different battery eliminators to operate gadgets like transistor sets, Audio Casette recorders and so on and so forth.

Materials required

- **Resistors and capacitors**
    - R_1 : 3.9 ohms, 2 watt
    - C_1 : 1000 µF, 25V (electrolytic)
    - C_2, C_3, C_4 : 0.1 µF (ceramic disc)
- **Semiconductor devices and ICs**
    - Diodes D_1 to D_4 : 1N4001 or equivalent
    - Zener diode V_{Z1} : 3V, 2 watt
    - IC_1 : 7812
    - IC_2 : 7809
    - IC_3 : 7806
- **Miscellaneous**
    - Transformer T_1 : 0-4, 5-7.5-12-15, 500 mA mains transformer
    - Fuse F_1 : Tubular type 500 mA fuse with holder
    - SW_2 : Main power ON/OFF switch
    - SW_1 : 3-pole, 4- throw rotatory switch

Power supply terminals, solder wire, mains cord etc.

Note : In case IC_2 and IC_3 are not easily available) IC_2 (7809) can be replaced by a 7805 with two series connected silicon diodes of 1N4001 type wired between the IC's common terminal and circuit GND.

IC_3 (7809) can also be replaced by a 7805 with a 3.9 zener diode wired from the IC's common terminal to circuit GND.

Assembly

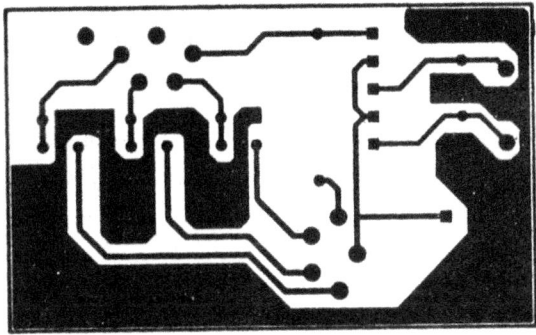

Fig. 17.1: Circuit Diagram

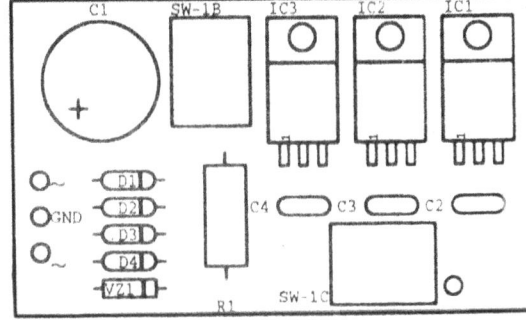

Fig. 17.2 : Circuit Diagram

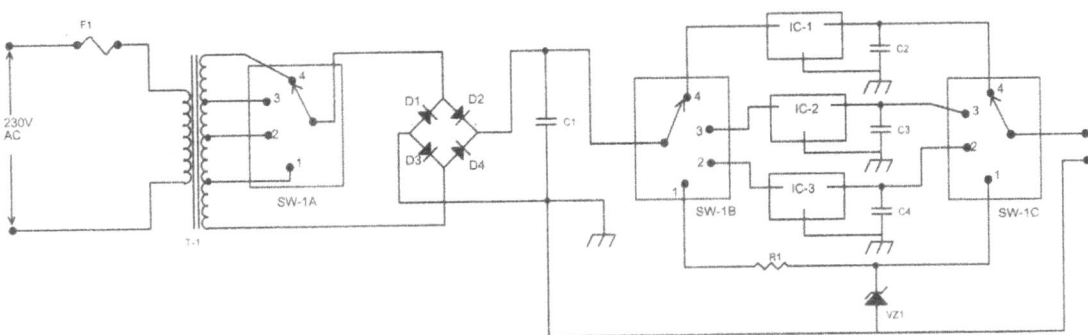

Fig. 17.3 : Circuit Diagram

The PCB layout and the components layout are respectively shown in fig. 17.1 and fig. 217.2.

The circuit shown in fig 17.3 comprises all the necessary circuit components needed for a conventional regulated power supply.

The transformer T-1 is a mains transformer with a multiple secondary winding that has taps at 4.5V, 7.5V ,12V and 15V. Switch SW1 is a 3 pole, 4-throw rotary switch and it has been shown as split up into three parts in the circuit diagram, the three parts being SW-1A, SW-1B and SW-1C. This switch can be used to select the desired output voltage. Diodes D_1 to D_4 constitute full wave bridge rectifier and capacitor C_1 is the filter capacitor.

IC-1, IC-2 and IC-3 are three terminal regulators of 78XX series. These regulators produce a fixed regulated output depending upon the type number chosen provided that the input to the regulator is at least 2.5V more than the expected output voltage. C_2 to C_4 are decoupling capacitors.

To Do and Notice
In observation this project should ensure that the output voltages have correct nominal values, they have the desired load current delivering capability and are nicely regulated.

What Happens?

The regulation part can be checked by varying the AC input to the power supply and monitoring the output voltage. Determine the input voltage range for which the output voltages maintain their values as constant.

Try It Yourself

Build a dual power supply that generates regulated +12 V and –12V from 220-230V AC mains.

Project-18

OP-AMP Tester

How can you test an opamp type 741 ?

Introduction

This test gadget can be used to test for general purpose opamp type 741 and other such opamps that are pin to pin compatible to 741. These include the opamp type numbers such as LM 709, LM 201, MC 1439, LM 748, OP-02, LM 318, LM 356 etc. With this gadget, we do not have to randomly replace the opamps in case the circuit we have built with so much enthusiam happens to use a few opamps and is not working. We will be able to test the opamp before declaring it fit for use.

Materials Required

R_1	:	470Ω, 1/2W carbon film resistor
R_2	:	1KΩ, 1/4W carbon film resistor
R_3	:	1Ω, 1/4W carbon film resistor
R_4	:	1KΩ, 1/4W carbon film resistor
R_5	:	2.2KΩ, 1/4W carbon film resistor
R_6	:	2.2KΩ, 1/4W carbon film resistor
C_1, C_2	:	100 µF/35 V electrolytic capacitors
C_3, C_4, C_5, C_6	:	0.1 µF ceramic capacitors
IC-1	:	Three terminal voltage regulator type 7812
IC-2	:	Three terminal voltage regulator type 7912
D_1 to D_4	:	IN4001 or equivalent diodes
LED-1 and LED-2	:	The two LEDs should preferably be of different colours
VZ-1	:	3V, 400 mW zener diode
T-1	:	Mains transformer (15-0-15, 250 mA)
SW-1	:	ON/OFF toggle switch
SW-2	:	DPDT switch
Fuse	:	500 mA
IC socket	:	8-pin DIL type

Assembly

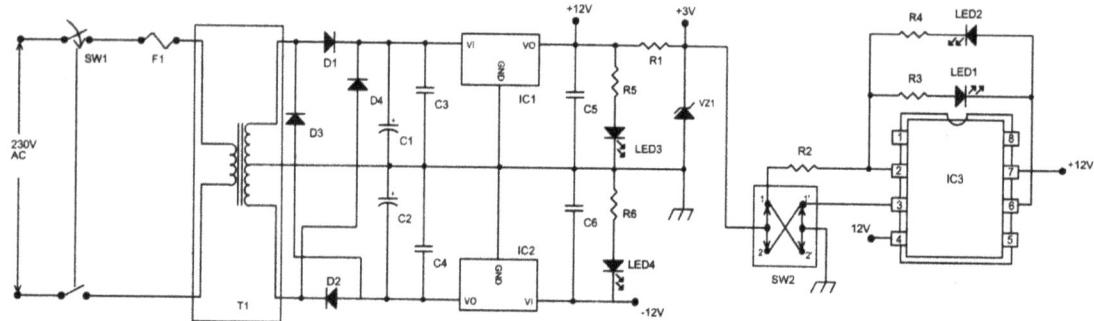

Fig. 18.1 : Circuit Diagram

A careful look at the circuit diagram will help you understand that the opamp under test can be wired either as an inverting amplifier (with gain equal to $R_{3/2}$) or as a non-inverting (with gain equal to $1 + R_4/R_2$) depending upon the position of the DPDT switch). The input to the amplifier in the two cases is a 3VDC. The circuit has its own regulated power supply to generate (+12V) and (−12V) for the opamp from the mains. The power supply circuit consists of a transformer with a center tapped secondary winding followed by a conventional full wave rectifier circuit for both positive as well as negative supplies. Diodes D_1 and D_4 constitute the full wave rectifier for the positive supply while the filtering action is provided by capacitor C_1.

Diode D_2 and D_3 provide rectification for generating the negative supply and capacitor C_2 does the filtering. 3V DC used as a test input to the opamp is generated by the R_1 and zener diode VZ-1.

To Do and Notice

1. Switch ON the test gadget. Measure the regulated +12V, −12V and +3V DC. Ensure that all the DC voltages are available.
2. Keep the DPDT switch (SW-2) in position 1-1.
3. Switch off the power supply.
4. Insert the opamp in the IC socket.
5. Switch on the power supply. LED-1 glows indicating that the inverting mode.
6. Change DPDT to position 2-2 LED-2 starts glowing, indicating the operation of opamp in non-inverting mode.
7. Switch off the power supply.

What Happens?

A bad opamp will not work in either of these configurations. But even if the opamp exhibits a behaviour where it works in one and not both of these configurations, it should still rated as a bad IC.

Try It Yourself

What do you know about the gain and CMRR ratio of an opamp ?

Project-19

Regulated Dual Power Supply

Can you build a dual power supply that generates +12 V and –12 V from 220-230 V AC mains?

Introduction
Some electronic circuits require a power supply with positive and negative outputs as well as zero volts. This is called dual supply because it is like two ordinary supplies connected together. Such a supply is a very common requirement in all those circuits that use opams.

Since opams are very widely used in a variety of circuits of hobbyists interests, construction of this project could serve as a very useful tool in testing all those circuits that need a dual supply. Each of the outputs in the circuit has a current delivering capability of 250 mA.

Materials Required

C_1, C_2	:	1000 µF, 50V electrolytic capacitor
C_3, C_4, C_7, C_8	:	0.1 µF ceramic disc capacitor
C_5, C_6	:	10 µF, 50V electrolytic capacitor
D_1 to D_4	:	1N4001 or equivalent diodes
IC-1	:	7812
IC-2	:	7912
SW-1	:	Mains ON/OFF switch
T-1	:	150-0-15V, 250 mA mains transformer
F-1	:	500 mA tubular type with holder fuse

Assembly
The unregualted AC/DC power supply part of the circuit consist of a transformer (T-1) that steps down 230V AC to 15V across a centre tapped secondary winding. Diodes D_1 to D_4 that rectify AC appearing across the secondary with D_1 and D_3 providing full wave rectification to produce positive output, D_2 and D_4 providing full wave rectification to produce a negative output, capacitor C_1 and C_2 providing the filtering action. C_3 to C_8 are decoupling capacitors. IC-1 is a fixed output positive three terminal regulator where IC-2 is a fixed output negative three terminal regulator.

Regulated Dual Power Supply

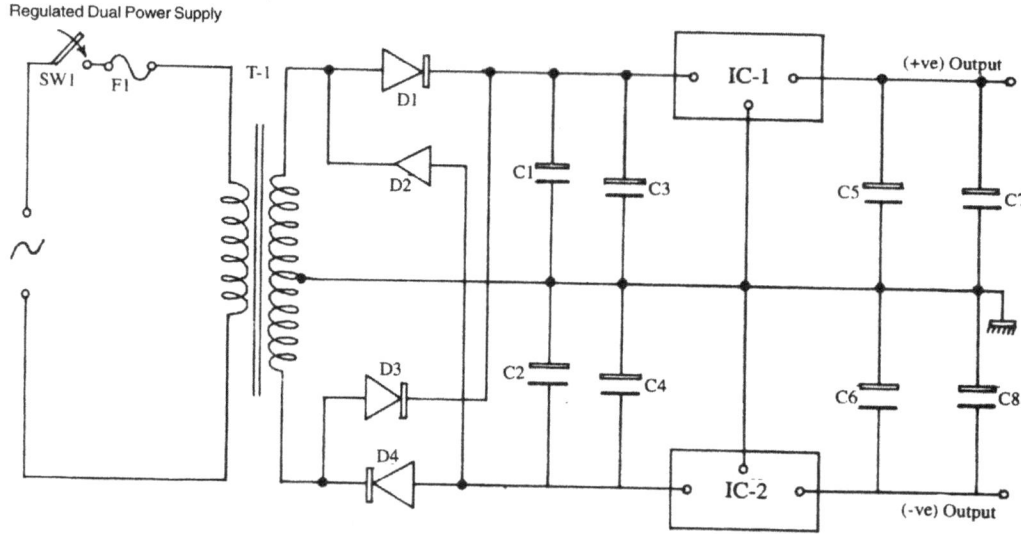

Fig 19.1 : Circuit Diagram

To Do and Notice

You have only switch ON the AC power and then measure the two output regulated voltages with a multimeter.

What Happens?

The load delivering-capability of supply can be verified by connecting a resistance of 47Ω, 5W across each of the two outputs as shown in the below figure and keep the circuit ON for ten to fifteen minutes.

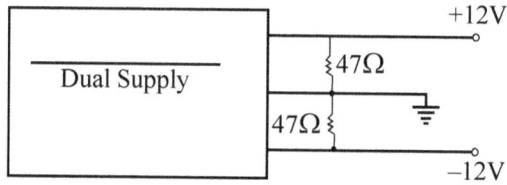

See that the transformer and IC regulators do not get excessively heated up and also that the regulated output voltage stay put. The regulated part can also be checked by feeding the AC input to the circuit from on VARIAC (variable auto transformer). You can verify that the DC outputs stay put at +12V and −12V for AC input right from 160 V to 320 V.

Try It Yourself

Use the same circuit configuration to produce (+ 5V, − 5V), (+ 9V, − 9V), (+ 15V, −15V).

Project-20

Single Pole, Double Throw Switch or 2-Way Switch

How do you control ON/OFF action of a lamp from two different places?

Introduction
While wiring a building, the multiway switching is the interconnection of two or more electrical switches to control an electrical load from more than one location. While a normal light switch needs to be only single-pole single-throw switch, the multiway switching requires the use of switches that have one or more additional contacts and two or more wires must be run beetween the switches. When the load is controlled from only two points, single-pole double-throw (SPDT) switches are used.

Materials Required
- Electric cable
- 6 drawing pins
- Two paper clips
- A 4.5V battery
- Two small tablets of wood
- A bulb and a bulb holder

Assembly
1. Push three drawing pins into each tablet of wood, as you see in the picture.
2. On each wooden tablet, open up a paper-clip and place one end under the centre drawing pin. In this way, the paper-clip can be moved to touch either of the other two drawing pins.
3. Using the electric cable, connect switches with the battery and the bulb, as shown in the fig.

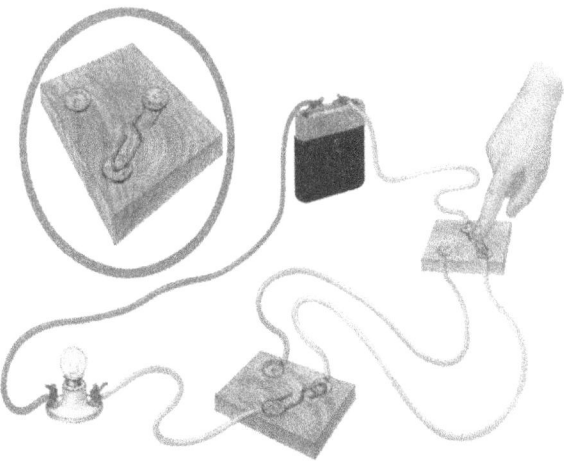

Fig. 20.1 : Circuit Diagram

4. Try different positions of the switches to light up or to extinguish the bulbs. You can understand the concept of electric switches in our home as : when a room has two doors, it may be necessary to switch the same light ON and OFF from different points for instance, near to each door. In this case, an electrical installation must be equipped with a two-way switches.

The same system can be used to switch the light ON or OFF both at the bottom and the top of a staircase.

To Do and Notice
The bulb can be lit or extinguished by either of the two switches.

What Happens?
When both switches and the wire form an unbroken circuit, the current passes through the circuit and the bulb lights up. Each time one of the two paper-clips is moved, this opens the circuit and makes the light go out.

Try It Yourself
Make 3-way switches and 4-way switches applying the above concept?

Project-21

Staircase Light with Auto-Switch-OFF Feature

Can you wire an electrical bulb with two switches with one of the switches placed at the bottom of a staircase and the other located at top?

Introduction

We are all familiar with the electrical wiring diagram. The wiring is done is such a way that either of the two switches can be used to switch ON the bulb (if it is initially OFF) or switch it OFF (if it is initially ON).

In the present circuit, we have two micro-switch with every push of either of the two switches the bulb lights up for a time period of about 40 seconds after that the light will turn automatically OFF.

Materials Required

- **Resistors**
  R_1, R_2, R_3, R_4 : 22K, 1/4W
  R_5, R_6 : 47K, 1/4W
  R_7 : 12K, 1/4W
  R_8 : 3.9K, 1/4W
  R_9 : 1.5K, 1/4W
  R_{10} : 4.70Ω, 1/4W
- **Capacitors**
  C_1, C_2, C_4 : 0.1 µF, 25V (ceramic disc)
  C_3, C_6 : 0.01 µF (ceramic disc)
  C_5 : 10 µF (Tantalum)
- **Semiconductor devices and ICs**
  Diodes D_1, D_2, D_3 : 1N4001
  Transistor Q_1 : 2N2222
  Voltage regulator, VR_1 : 7805
  IC_1, IC_2 : CD4011
  IC_3 : timer 555
- **Hardware components**
  SW_1, SW_2 : Micro-switches
  SW_3 : ON/OFF toggle switch

RL₁ : 9V DC/100 to 200Ω relay with at least one normally open (NO) contact
L₁ : Suitable 230V AC bulb 40 to 100 watt rating
Multistand wires, solder metal, general purpose PCB (if required)

Assembly

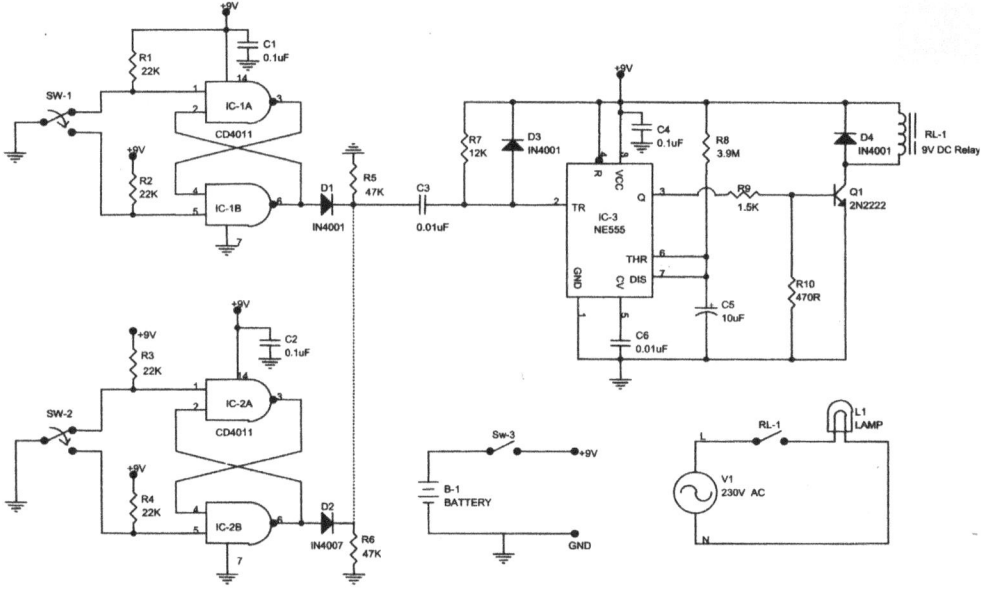

Fig. 21.1 : Circuit Diagram

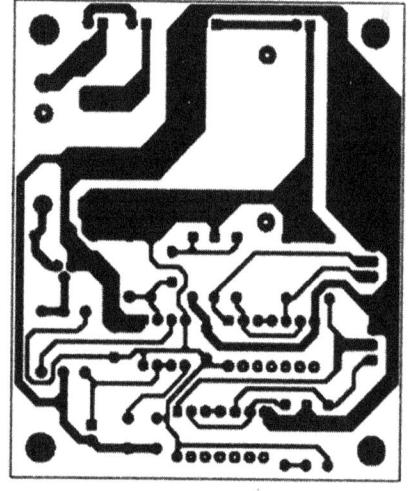

Fig. 21.2 : Circuit Diagram

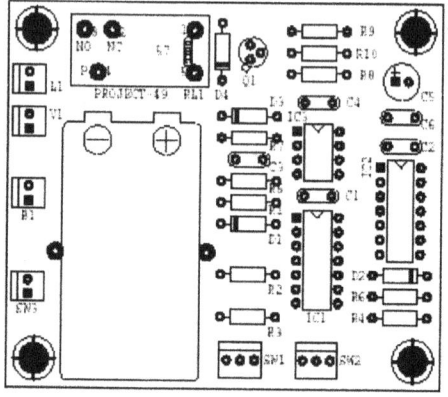

Fig. 21.3 : Circuit Diagram

Staircase Light with Auto-Switch-OFF Feature

Fig. 21.1 shows the circuit diagram. SW_1 and SW_2 are the two micro-switches, which feed the inputs of their respective de-bouncing circuits. Each de-bouncing circuit is built around the famous back-to-back connection of two NAND gates. The de-bouncing circuit ensures a clean bounce free pulse at the output every time the micro switch is pressed.

Fig. 21.2 and 21.3 show the PCB layout and components layout diagrams respectively. From these diagrams, it should not be difficult for you to make your own PCB and then place the components at their designated places. In real practice, if you have to actually implement the device in your house, you would need to make separate PCBs for the two switches along with their de-bouncing circuits and another PCB for the control circuit.

To Do and Notice

The two switches should located physically apart at some distance, we have used separate NAND gate ICs (CD4011) for each debouncing circuit. The outputs from the two de-bouncing circuits are O red using diodes, D_1 (IN4001) and D_2 (IN4001). So every time we press either of the micro-switches, we get a positive pulse at the junction of cathodes of diodes D_1 and D_2. This pulse is used to trigger the monoshot circuit configured around IC_3 (Timer IC 555). The triggering occurs on the trailing edge of the pulse. The output of monostat goes high for a time given by 1.1R and C_5. The time period for the chosen values is 40 seconds. The 40 second pulse drives the transistor Q_1 (2N2222) wired as a switch. The realy RL_1 gets activated thus closing the normally open relay contact wired in series with the mains and the bulb.

What Happens?

The bulb extinguishes when the relay gets de-activated after 40 seconds period has elapsed. Diode D_4 (IN4001) is to protect the transistor Q_1 against transients during relay switch-OFF operation.

The circuit operates on 9V DC derived from a battery, which gets connected to the circuit through a toggle switch SW_3. In the actual setup, this DC voltage could also be derived from AC mains voltage.

Try It Yourself

Make an electrical arrangement to get a similar facility.

Project-22

Temperature Switch

Do you have understanding of the use of germanium diode and silicon diode ?

Introduction

This temperature switch project will provide you with an understanding of how to use of germanium diode and how it works compared to the more common silicon diode. It works on the principle that as the temperature surrounding the germanium diode increases, the back resistance decreases sharply.

Materials Required

Q_1, Q_2	:	BC 548 NPN transistor
Q_3	:	2 SC2002 NPN transistor
R_1	:	120 kΩ, 1/4W 5% carbon film resistor
R_2	:	1 kΩ, 1/4W 5% carbon film resistor
VR_1	:	1 MΩ potentiometer
D_1	:	Germanium diode
D_2, D_3	:	1N4003 diode
BZ	:	12 Buzzer

Assembly

The schematic of the project is shown in fig 22.1. It uses only 10 components to illustrate the understanding of germanium diode and its characteristics. This project is suitable for beginners to electronics and will definitely help to inculcate the interest in designing electronic projects.

You can use any equivalent NPN and PNP transistors to replace BC548 and 2SC 2002 respectively as these parts may not be freely available in our country.

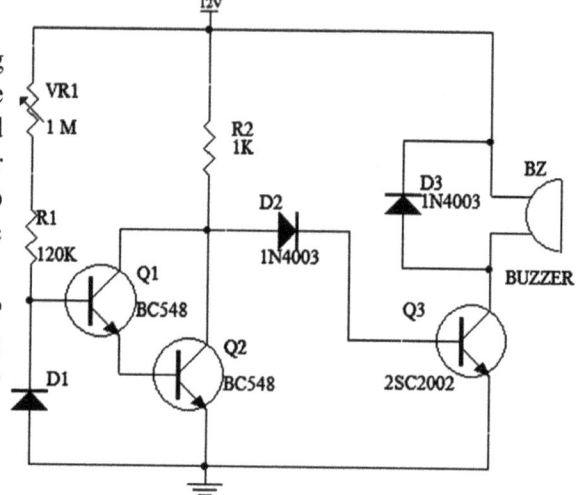

Fig. 22.1 : Circuit Diagram

Temperature Switch

To Do and Notice
At room temperature, the buzzer is OFF. When the temperature of the surrounding increases, the buzzer is ON indicating that ambient temperature has risen.

What Happens?
At room temperature, the germanium diode D_1 has a typical back resistance of $10\ k\Omega$. At this value the base of transistor Q_1 is turned ON, causing transistor Q_2 to be turned ON as well. When this happens, the base transistor Q_3 is kept to ground causing it to turn OFF; hence, the buzzer is OFF.

When the temperature of the surrounding increases, the back resistance of the germanium diode D_1 decreases sharply causing the base of transistor Q_1 to pull down near ground potential. This cause the transistor Q_1 and Q_2 to turn OFF. Transistor Q_3 is now forward bias through resistor R_2 and diode D_2. This causes the buzzer to turn ON indicating that the ambient temperature has risen. The sensitivity of the circuit can be adjusted by adjusting variable resistor VR_1 and subjecting diode D_1 to a temperature that will trigger the buzzer.

Try It Yourself
Draw the V-I curve for germanium and silicon diodes and show the effect of temperature on these diodes.

Project-23

Touch Switch

How to make a LED ON or OFF by a physical touch ?

Introduction
In this project a CMOS quad 2 input NOR gate IC is used as a latching circuit to switch a LED ON and OFF by physically touching the ON metal plate or OFF metal plate. The CD4001BC integrated circuit is a monolithic complementary MS (CMOS) IC that are constructed with N- and P- channel enhancement mode transistors. Its input are protected against electrostatic discharge with diodes to VDD and VSS.

Materials Required

U_1	:	Quad 2 input NOR gate CMOS CD4001BC
LED	:	Light emitting diode
R_1	:	3.3M Ω 1/4W, 5% resistor
R_2	:	3.3M Ω 1/4W, 5% resistor
R_3	:	10 kΩ 1/4W, 5% resistor
R_4	:	470 kΩ 1/4W, 5% resistor
R_5	:	10 kΩ 1/4W, 5% resistor
C_1	:	0.1 µF/25V ceramic capacitor
BAT	:	9V battery with holder
T_1, T_2, T_3, T_4	:	Touch terminal
Q_1	:	PNP transistor 2SA953

Touch Switch

Assembly

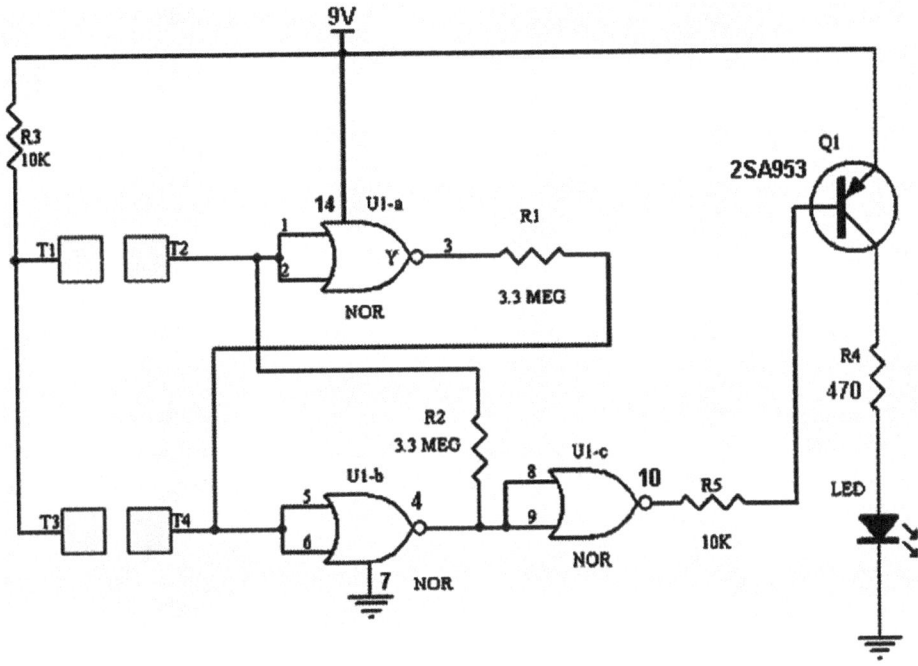

Fig. 23.1 : Circuit Diagram

The circuit shown in fig 23.1 shows the schematic diagram of the touch circuit of which the NOR gates are configured as a simple latching circuit.

To Do and Notice
When the skin contact is made between T_1 and T_2 or T_3 and T_4, the LED switches ON and OFF respectively. The latching circuit ensures that the output will not fluctuate between ON and OFF.

What Happens?
When T_1 and T_2 contacts are bridged through the skin contact, the output U_1-a will go to logic '0' and cause the output of U_1-b to go to logic '1'. This output will in turn cause NOR gate U_1-C to go to logic '0' causing transistor Q_1 to turn ON, and hence LED will turn ON.

The circuit will remain latched with the LED ON until contacts T_3 and T_4 are bridged of which the output of U_1-a will go to logic '1', output of U_1-b will go to logic '0', output of U_1-c will go to logic '1' and transistor Q_1 will turn OFF. The LED will then turn OFF.

Try It Yourself
Make a remote controlled ON/OFF switch.

Project-24

Transistor Tester

Can you make a tester circuit to test the bipolar junction transistor both PNP and NPN ?

Introduction
This project is a simple circuit that can be used to test BJT transistors. In addition to testing the transistors for any defect. This easy to build test gadget can also be used to measure the (hFE) at a given healthy transistor.

Two different sets of three terminals each have been brought out on the front panel, one for testing NPN and the other for testing PNP transistors. Also (hFE) measurement can be carried out for a wide range of transistors starting with low (hFE) power transistors to high (hFE) small signal transistors. An (hFE) as high as 1000 can be measured with this gadget.

Materials Required

R_1	:	1KΩ, 1/4 W carbon film resistor
R_2, R_3	:	470KΩ, 1/4 W carbon film resistor
P_1, P_2	:	100KΩ, preset potentiometers
VZ-1, VZ-2	:	5.6V, 400 mW zener diodes
Q_1	:	2N2907 PNP transistor
Q_2	:	2N2222 NPN
S_1	:	ON/OFF switch
Battery	:	9V battery

Assembly
The heart of the circuit has two constant current sources built around transistors (Q_1) and (Q_2). Q_1 is a PNP transistor.

To Do and Notice
If the transistor under test is NPN, then provide current by Q_1 circuit. If the transistor under test in PNP provide current by Q_2-circuit. The constant current is fed to the base of transistor under test. This current is multiplied by the (h_{FE}) of the transistor under test and flows in the collector which is

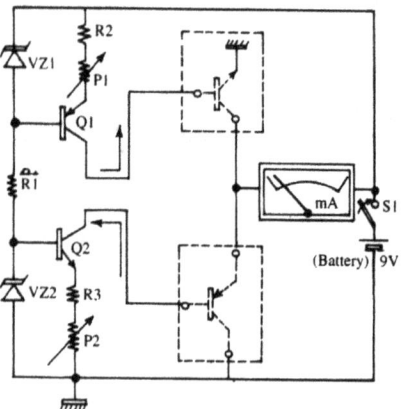

Fig. 24.1 : Circuit Diagram

indicated by the meter.

This is true as the transistor under test is always operaing in the non-saturated mode.

What Happens?

Q_1 is a PNP transistor and the constant current flows in the emitter lead. The same constant current flows out of the collector lead. The magnitude of constant current is given by :

$$\frac{VZ-1-0.6}{(R_2+P_1)}$$

P_1 is adjusted to get a constant current of 10 µA. The second current source is built around NPN transistor (Q_2) and the magnitude of constant current is given by :

$$\frac{VZ-2-0.6}{(R_3+P_2)}$$

Again P_2 is adjusted to get a constant current of 10µA.

Here almost same constant current flows into the collector lead of Q_2. Minimum value of (h_{FE}) that can be measured depends upon the full scale deflection of the meter. The meter can infact be directly calibrated to read the (h_{FE}) of the transistor. The (h_{FE}) check provides an automatic check for the functioning of the transistor.

Try It Yourself

How do you identify a transistor leads? Does the terminal identification changes for NPN and PNP transistors.

Project-25

USB Mobile Charger Circuit

Can you make a USB mobile charger ?

Introduction

We can use this circuit to charge a mobile while we are going on a journey. So, we may treat it as mobile travel charger circuit.

The USB part of the mobile is used for charging as the USB port is very helpful voltage source that can charge the mobile. Nowadays, there are two to four USB ports on the laptops that are available in the market. USB actually refers to Universal Serial Bus. It is the newest method which is used to get information in and out from your computer. We are concerned with the fact that ± 5V of power is being provided by the USB port to external devices and can avail at the pin-1 while on pin-4, it is 0 V, till 100 mA of current we can get from the USB port which is more than sufficient that we require for this small application.

Materials Required

R_1	:	470 Ω, 1% resistor
C_1	:	100 µF/25V capacitor
T_1	:	BC 547 transistor
Zener diode	:	4.7V/0.5 W
Diode	:	1N4007
USB	:	Cables

Assembly

The figure 25.2 shows the circuit diagram. Resistors are used to control the circuit current. Capacitors are mainly used to store charges, electrolytic capacitor is an example of polarized while ceramic and paper capacitors are non-polarised. Zener diode starts working at breakdown point. It works always in reverse bias state.

The circuit explained above works on 4.7 regulated voltage. The voltage at output is harmonised by the transistor named T-1.

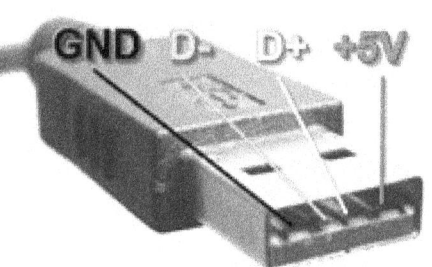

Fig. 25.1 : USB Port

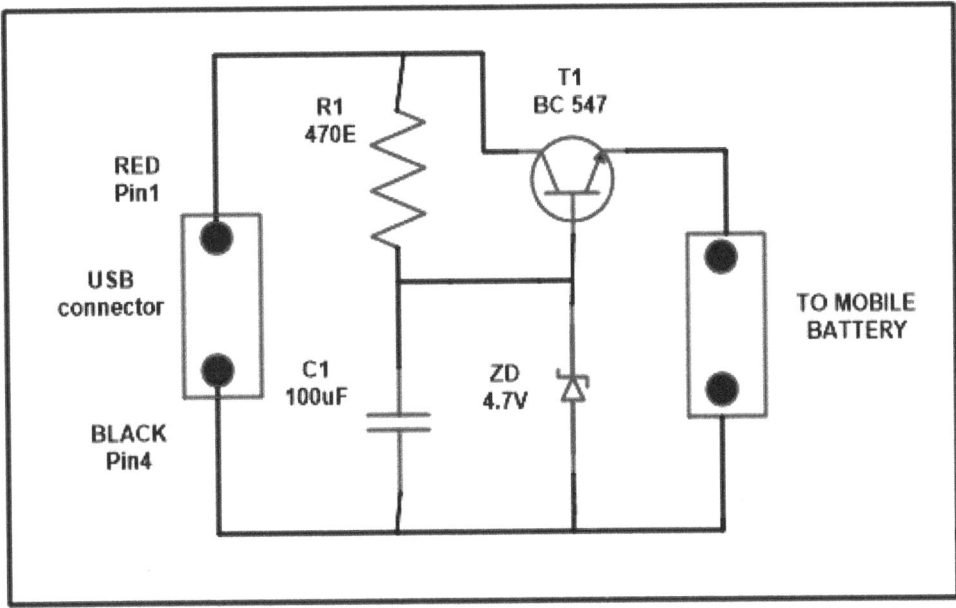

Fig. 25.2 : Circuit Diagram

To Do and Notice
The USB cables are made up of wires. The back colour wire is negative while the red colour wire is positive. 5V is the voltage that we get from USB port. And more than 500 mA current can not be supplied to the device that is attached to the USB port.

Attach the power line with USB plug and examine the right polarity.

What Happens?
The large number of mobile battries work on 3.6V, 1000 to 13000 mAh. These batteries are combinations of three lithium cells whose voltage rating is 1.2V for each. And for charging mobile quickly, there is a need of 4.5 volt and current range of 300-500 mA.

The USB cable used in this project has minimum one male plug with strip back of about 5 cm having external padding safeguard from the 'uncovered' end of the USB cable.

Try It Yourself
Try to know the need of diode in above project?

Project-26

Variable Power Supply and Charger

Can you make a mobile phone battery charger with emergency light ?

Introduction

This is very easy circuit of 'variable power supply and charger'. It is not very much useful in the time of power cut but can be used as main power supply. At your workbench you can use this circuit to check or test your electronic projects. Mobile phone batteries can be changed with the help of these circuits.

This circuit can also work as an emergency light.

Materials Required

IC	:	LM 317
R_1	:	220Ω, 1% carbon film resistor
R_2 to R_{12}	:	220Ω, 1% carbon film resistor
R_{13}	:	470Ω, 1% carbon film resistor
VR-1	:	100KΩ variable resistor
C_1	:	100 µF capacitor
C_2	:	0.1 µF capacitor
D_1 to D_4	:	IN4005 diodes
S_1 to S_5	:	ON/OFF switches
LED_1 to LED_{12}	:	LEDs
Zener diode	:	3.3V
Transforer and battery		

Assembly

As per your need you can take the output from the circuit by just flipping different number of switches (from S_3, S_4 and S_5) in the circuit. S_1 and S_2 are the two switches that are given in the circuit so that you can power your circuit either directly with the AC supply or else you can take help of any battery.

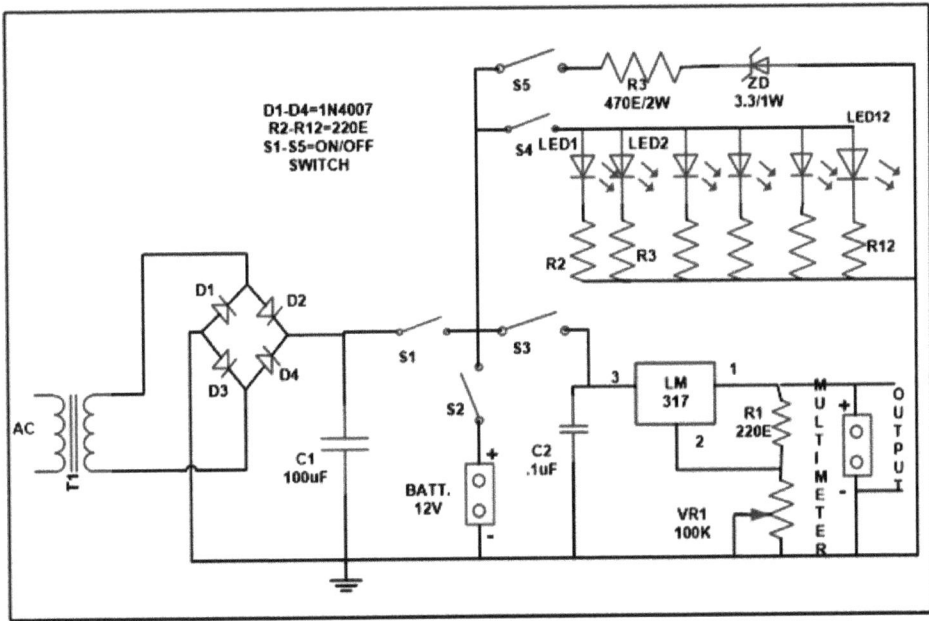

Fig. 26.1 : Circuit Diagram

To Do and Notice
With the help of flipping S_5 switch which is provided in the circuit Li-ions battery can be charged, which are generally used in the mobile phones with the assist of your mobile connectors. Turn over to switch S_5 if you want to use the emergency light.

In place of AC power supply, solar panels can be used and for storing charge, you can take rechargeable batteries. This will not merely save electric bill but also assist you a lot in the state of power failure.

What Happens?
If you require the variable power supply as your output then, set the switch S_3 into 'ON-state'. LM 317 is used in the circuit which is a variable voltage regulator to supply variable power. The LM 317 is basically positive voltage regulator and has three terminals. 1.2V to 37 V is the range of the output voltage that is provided by the LM 317. Different ranges of voltage can be achieved by just adjusting the variable resistor that is provided in the circuit and with the help of multimeter, the output can be seen and the voltage which is desireble can be set. The power supply range can alter from 1.5 V to 12.V. If you want to use an AC supply, then flip to switch S_1 while if you want to supply from the battery then flip to switch S_2.

Try It Yourself
Try to make an automatic street light controller circuit.

Project-27

Water Sensor

How do you make water sensor alarm system?

Introduction

A sensor is a converter that measures a physical quantity and converts it into a signal which can be read by an observer or by an electronic instrument. A sensor's sensitivity indicates how much the sensor's output changes when the measured quantity changes. In this project, we use a transistor to amplify the signal from humidity (water) sensor.

Materials Required

30 pF capacitor (water-vapour sensor) two N-P-N transistors, two 100 KΩ, one 300Ω and one 330Ω reistors, 9 V lantern battery, plug-in board, connecting wires, battery clip, red LED, 100 KΩ, variable resistor, screw driver and auto range digital multimeter.

Assembly

Humidity sensor works through electrical conductivity, when water vapour condenses on the plates, it forms a thin film that conducts electricity between the two plates. In that case the water sensor is like a resistor except its resistance value changes depending on the amount of water in the air. It is made by cliping the top of a 30 pF capacitor using a pair of wire clippers.

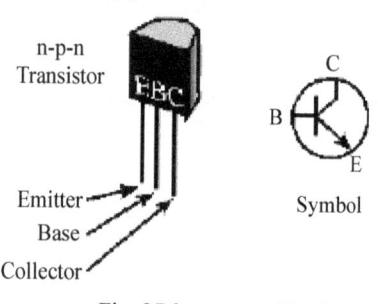

Fig. 27.1 Fig. 27.2

Transistor connections: Our kit contains a N-N-P transistor which has emitter, base and collector terminals. The collector and emitter are connected to a pipe that carries water and base connected to faucet (a device that controls flow of water from the pipe).

Ordinarily the base is closed and the resistance between collector and emitter is very large. When a small voltage is applied to the base, it reduces the resistance between the collector and emitter, allowing the flow of current.

Wiring up the water sensor: The circuit diagram is shown at right and experimental arrangement of the water sensor in the above figure.

Test the circuit with the multimeter on "VDC" (Volts Direct Current) setting, touch the sensor with your finger. The voltage reading should change. A change in the voltage reading indicates a change in the humidity of the air around the sensor. This circuit is sensitive enough to detect the water vapour.

Adding over limit Alarm

Now, we will add a red LED to the above circuit as an over-limit

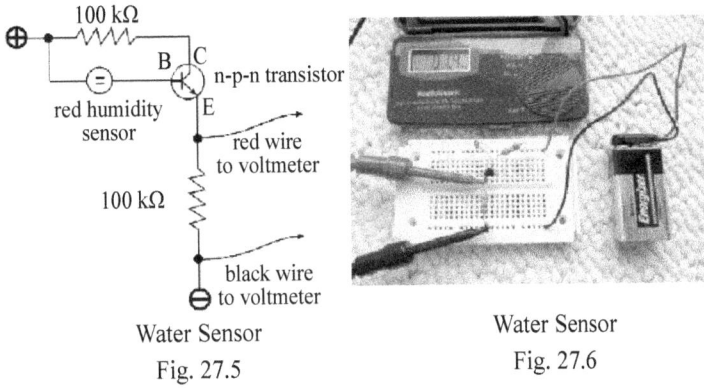

Water Sensor
Fig. 27.5

Water Sensor
Fig. 27.6

alarm. The LED will light up when the sensor detects a high amount of water vapour. The circuit diagram is shown below. One more n-p-n transistor is added to the circuit which will drive the LED. The voltage signal output from the first transistor is sent to the base of the second transistor.

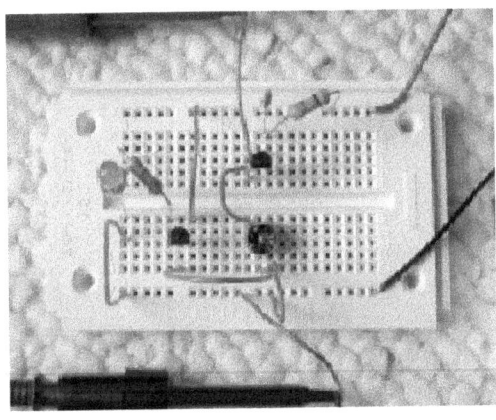

Fig. 27.7 : Water sensor circuit with over limit indicator (Red LED)

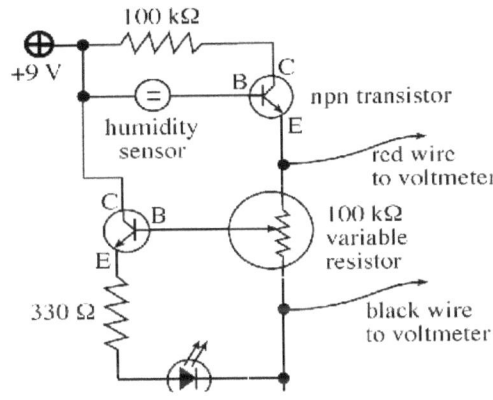

Fig. 27.8 : Circuit diagram

The circuit also incorporates a 100 KΩ variable resistor in place of one of the 100 KΩ resistor. The variable resistor allows you to set the threshold level for the over-limit alarm.

To Do and Notice

The red-LED should light up when you touch the sensor with your fingertip or get it wet with a drop of water. You will be able to adjust the threshold level where the red light glows. Adjust the dial on the variable resistor using a small screwdriver.

What Happens?

Sensors are just like transducer there. The sensor used senses the humidity and generates an electrical signal which initiates the circuit and red LED glows.

Try It Yourself

Implement this project in your home. By doing this you will be able to stop wastage of water. Instead of LED you can also use a buzzer alarm.

❐

QUIZ BOOKS

ENGLISH IMPROVEMENT

ACTIVITIES BOOK

QUOTES/SAYINGS

BIOGRAPHIES

CHILDREN SCIENCE LIBRARY

IELTS TECH

COMPUTER BOOKS

Also available in Hindi   Also available in Hindi

All books available at www.vspublishers.com

STUDENT DEVELOPMENT/LEARNING

POPULAR SCIENCE

Also Available in Hindi

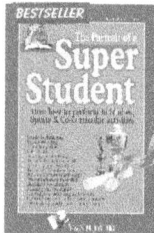   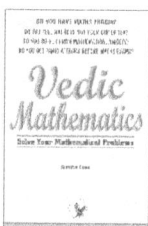  
Also Available in Hindi

Also Available in Hindi   Also Available in Hindi

PUZZLES

Also Available in Hindi   Also Available in Hindi, Tamil & Bangla

DRAWING BOOKS

CHILDREN'S ENCYCLOPEDIA - THE WORLD OF KNOWLEDGE

  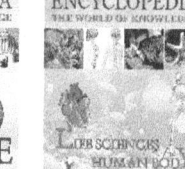   

Contact us at sales@vspublishers.com

GENERAL HEALTH & BEAUTY CARE | MISCELLANEOUS

FITNESS

PERFECT HEALTH & AYURVEDA

     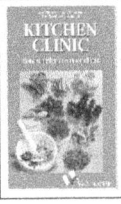 

A Set of 4 Books

DISEASES & COMMON AILMENTS

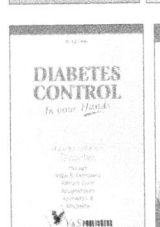    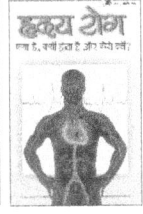 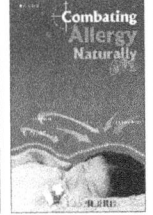 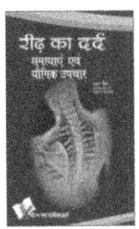

REGIONAL LANGUAGE

      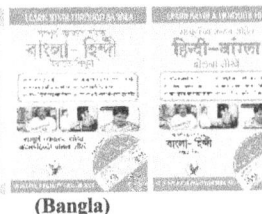

(Telugu)　　(Odia)　　(Marathi)　　(Bangla)

All books available at www.vspublishers.com

CONCISE DICTIONARIES

ACADEMIC BOOKS

Available in Paperback & Pocket size also

ENGLISH DICTIONARIES

HINDI DICTIONARIES

Available in Pocket size also

ENGLISH DICTIOANRIES

Available in Pocket size also

 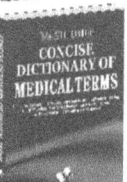  

FICTION

Contact us at sales@vspublishers.com

www.ingramcontent.com/pod-product-compliance
Lightning Source LLC
Chambersburg PA
CBHW080448110426
42743CB00016B/3320